Did you hear about the Russia...

... who fell in ...
bought her a pre...
year's supply of le...

who made a perfect three-point landing . . .
in a kite.

who thought "panty raid" was what his girl
friend sprayed in her undies . . .

who wanted to be an Indian, so he bought a
"bow" tie and an "Arrow" shirt.

> Ivan, Ivan, sat on a wall.
> Ivan, Ivan, had a great fall.
> All the king's horsemen
> Thought he was dead.
> But lucky for Ivan
> He lit on his head.

Hollywood is going to do a new epic movie
called Flea Circus starring actual fleas. It'll be
a low-budget film. All they have to do is hire
one Russian and he'll provide them with a cast
of thousands.

Also by Steve Leininger:

The Official Ukrainian Joke Book

The Official Russian Joke Book

Steve Leininger

PINNACLE BOOKS   NEW YORK

To Charlie . . . my best friend!

THE OFFICIAL RUSSIAN JOKE BOOK

An original Pinnacle Books edition, published for the first time anywhere.

First printing, March 1981

ISBN: 0-523-41427-7

Cover and interior illustration by Ron Wing

Printed in the United States of America

PINNACLE BOOKS, INC.
1430 Broadway
New York, New York 10018

CONTENTS

1. Comrades at Arms

Why are Siberian guards considered to be so unfriendly?
Because they have such icy stares.

* * *

Are Russian soldiers tough?
Not if you cook them slowly and use a little meat tenderizer.

* * *

A guard near the wall of Berlin
Was told to let nobody in.
He let one girl through
For a favor or two.
And now he's locked up in the pen!

A troop of cossacks was scouting for signs of enemy cavalry. The lead rider jumped from his mount and put his ear to the ground. In a few moments he pulled a notebook from inside his tunic and, placing his ear once more to the ground, began writing furiously.

"Well?" asked the troop leader. "Do you hear anything?"

"Let's see," said the cossack as he surveyed his notes. "An earthworm going to bed, two rattlesnakes having a domestic quarrel, a prairie dog with gas, two maggots making love, but no hoofbeats."

* * *

Why do Russian soldiers have black shiny boots?

Their diapers leak.

* * *

A Russian soldier was given a special mission. "Private!" said his commanding officer. "I want to get in that jeep and drive across into the free zone and scout the positions of the capitalist pigs!"

The poor soldier had only driven 20 yards into Allied territory when two jet fighters swooped down and fired their rockets. When the smoke had cleared, he looked up to see six huge tanks bearing down on him. In his hurry to escape, he lost control of the jeep and turned it over four times and landed in a roadside ditch. He managed to crawl back to his own side of the border where he found his commanding officer waiting for a report.

"Well?" demanded the officer. "Did you find the capitalist pigs?"

"No pigs, sir!" gasped the private. "But I came across the worst horde of road hogs I ever hope to meet!"

* * *

Guard #1: "I found a suspicious character near the wall yesterday, and when I asked what he was doing he didn't answer me. He just stared at me and refused to talk."

Guard #2: "What did you do?"

Guard #1: "I set fire to the bassinet."

* * *

Here lies a fair Russian lassie
Who thought that escape would be classy.
She stumbled and sank
'Neath the treads of a tank
And now she's part of the chassis.

* * *

How does a Russian soldier prepare for a gas attack?

He unpacks three cans of beans and a 3-speed fan.

Russian tank: A bulldozer, a box of fire crackers, and a slingshot.

* * *

Russian submarine: A canoe full of big rocks and a snorkel.

* * *

Russian aircraft carrier: A Ball dome jar full of flies with cherry bombs taped to their backs.

* * *

Russian armor-piercing shell: An arrow with a canopener head.

* * *

The president of the US was concerned about the nation's ability to hit back in case of a nuclear attack. Deciding that striking the Soviet population centers would be the best strategy, he called in his chiefs of staff.

"Where would you say is the largest concentration of Russians?" asked the president.

"In hell, sir!" was the unanimous reply.

Russian naval destroyer: A belt with a nail in it.

* * *

Did you hear about the Russian special force who was going to launch an air strike against Florida?
Their blowguns got plugged up with goo in the Everglades.

* * *

Why are people with no arms and legs drafted into the Russian army?
They're cheaper than sandbags.

* * *

Russian poison gas grenade: A belch-in-a-bottle!

* * *

Then there was the Russian soldier who was told to put up a smoke screen.
The government reimbursed his survivors $3,000 for the cigars and gave him a Purple Heart for lung cancer.

"Stop complaining! You chose the weapons. I chose the place!"

How does a Russian drill sergeant holler cadence while marching?

Left, left, left, left! Left, left, left, left!

* * *

Why don't Russian sharpshooters have itchy trigger fingers?

Because they're all thumbs.

* * *

Russian tanks may look ominous but under all that paint they all say "Tonka."

* * *

How did the crew of the sunken Russian submarine die?

Trying to launch the lifeboats.

* * *

Natasha: "Oh, Boris, darlink! Don't join army! They make you 'Gay'!"

Boris: "Ha! How they make macho man like me 'Gay'?"

Natasha: "Have you no heard? They make you parade in 'dress' uniform!"

General: "Do you have any last requests before we take you out and shoot you?"

Prisoner: "Yes. Could I finish reading *War and Peace*? I'm already on page 3!"

* * *

How can you recognize a Russian infantry division?

Fire one shot in the air. If 1,000 white flags pop out, it's Russian!

* * *

Igor: "During World War II my Uncle Petrovich was surrounded by a patrol of 50 German soldiers."

Ivan: "What did he do?"

Igor: "He played possum."

Ivan: "Oh, then he escaped?"

Igor: "No, he fell out of the tree six times."

* * *

Why does the Russian army draft 93-100-year-old men?

So they can strip them naked, paint them brown, and send them into the French vineyards disguised as raisins.

Two Russian soldiers were at a bar guzzling vodka.

"Tell me," asked the first. "Could you hit an enemy soldier at 100 yards with just one shot?"

"Not with one shot," replied the second. "But give me a whole bottle of this stuff and I'll wipe out their entire army!"

* * *

Do they have a "Mission Impossible" type force in the Soviet Union?

Yes, but it's more sophisticated than ours. Their tape recorders do not self-destruct in 5 seconds. Their agents do!

* * *

Igor: "Uncle Petrovich is really feeling run down lately."

Ivan: "What got him? A flu bug?"

Igor: "No, an Army tank."

Ivan: "Why would a tank run over Uncle Petrovich?"

Igor: "They were trying to *press* him into the service."

* * *

How do you keep the Russian army from shelling your position?

Shoot at their chickens.

How do you keep the Russian army from overrunning your position?

Aim for their white-tipped canes.

* * *

Instructions for Russian flame thrower: *Close cover before striking!*

* * *

It is true that the Russians are ahead of us in the arms race. For instance, when a Russian girl has to get married her father shows up at the wedding with a 10 megaton bomb instead of a shotgun.

* * *

Igor: "I heard your uncle got shot today trying to escape the country. Are you going to the service?"

Ivan: "Naw, I already been in the army once."

* * *

What do you call a Russian expert in hand-to-hand combat that attacks a soldier holding a flame thrower?

A second-degree blackbelt with third-degree burns.

How do you stop a Russian amphibious landing?

Aim for their rubber horsies.

Russia lost all of her 400,000 intelligent citizens last week. A border guard fell asleep and they all snuck home to Poland.

*   *   *

Then there was the Russian soldier on the grenade range who pulled the wrong pin and his diaper exploded.

*   *   *

What should you do if a Russian soldier attacks your rear?
Be patient. He'll be through in a minute or two.

*   *   *

Kid: "Were you really in Stalingrad during the siege, Daddy?"
Dad: "Yep, sure was."
Kid: "Wow! What did you eat?"
Dad: "Rats mostly."
Kid: "Boy! That must have been tough."
Dad: "As a matter of fact, they were surprisingly tender with a little roasting."

*   *   *

What do you call a Russian sharpshooter?
A Marx-man.

A Russian general had several Nazis trapped on a hill. He called his sergeant over and asked:

"What do you think? Can we take the crest?"

"I dunno," answered the soldier. "We can take their canteens maybe, but they guard their toothpaste with their lives!"

* * *

Then there was the Russian sailor who fell in love with a mermaid and bought her a present to impress her . . . a year's supply of leg make-up."

* * *

Two Russian soldiers were chased by the enemy into a barren desert.

"This is a fine fix!" mumbled the first. "It's at least a 100 degrees out and a good 2-day walk to the nearest water hole."

"Don't worry!" beamed the second. "We no be thirsty long!"

"You have water?"

"Naw! But I have thirteen packages of Kool-aid!"

* * *

Is Russian housing run down?

Only when the army goes on tank maneuvers.

Why did King Arthur kick out his only Russian knight?

He kept sticking his bubble gum under the round table.

* * *

Why didn't Sir Lancelot ever accept a challenge from a Russian knight?

He couldn't bring himself to stab a guy wearing a garbage can for armor.

* * *

Then there was the Russian plane with 200 troopers aboard. It developed engine trouble and the pilot insisted that all unnecessary, useless equipment be thrown out the door. It's the worst case of mass mutual castration in history!

* * *

A Russian general was visiting a field hospital during World War II. His job was to cheer up the wounded troops and boost their morale. At one point on his tour he entered the tent of 40-some soldiers who had at least one leg amputated. His aide whispered, "Sir, the men are waiting to hear some words of encouragement. Haven't you anything to say?"

After looking around the ward and thinking for a few minutes, the general cleared his throat and said, "Keep your chins up, men! You never know when the Kremlin may need actors for a pirate movie."

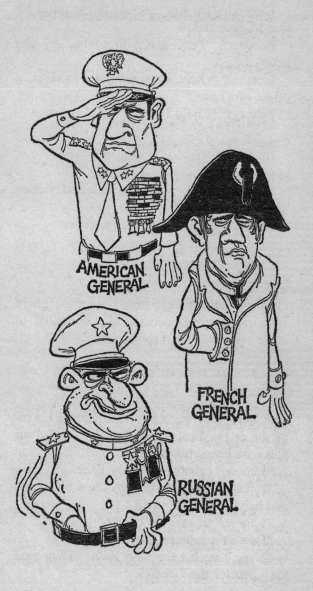

AMERICAN GENERAL

FRENCH GENERAL

RUSSIAN GENERAL

General: "Do you have any last requests before we shoot you?

Prisoner: "Yes. I'd like to confess my sins before I die."

General: "Okay, do you want a minister, a priest, or a rabbi?"

Prisoner: "Could I have a nun?"

* * *

Why were the Russians defeated during World War I?

They kept falling out of the trenches.

* * *

Then there was the sexy girl prison guard who quit her job because she was tired of being everybody's last meal.

* * *

A naval aide burst into the office of his superior at the Pentagon. "Sir," he cried, "our files have been broken into!"

"I know," calmly replied the Exec.

"But they'll be able to copy those blueprints and build ships like ours!"

"I know," yawned the officer.

"Doesn't it concern you at all, sir?"

"Nope," smiled the navy man. "They took the plans for the *Titanic*!"

The Russians are always displaying their missiles and making threats. How do they expect to instill in us a sense of fear when they can't instill in themselves a sense of anything?

* * *

Are Russians good at breaking codes?
Only if you write them on a sheet of glass and then they have to use a hammer.

* * *

What do you call eight Russian soldiers parachuting from an airplane over cannibal country?
Food drop!

* * *

Submarine Captain: "Up scope!"
Sailor: "Yeah! I tried that stuff and it didn't help my breath either!"

* * *

Then there was the Russian aviator who made a perfect three-point landing . . . in a kite.

German veterans of World War II have some frightening stories to tell about their experiences in Russia. One of the most terrible was spending the night on the Russian plains. As soon as the sun went down the night air was filled with horrifying mournful howls. It wasn't coyotes baying at the moon. It was Russian soldiers who went out to pee trying to zip up their trousers in the dark.

* * *

Captain: "How did Private Trotskovich die?"

Sergeant: "He was on the bazooka range with Private Boris. Boris had the bazooka and Trotskovich was loading it."

Captain: "So? What happened?"

Sergeant: "He shoved the shell in the back of the bazooka and tapped him on the shoulder. Boris turned around to see what he wanted, and Boom!"

* * *

Soldier: "Sir! The prison is on fire and 500 political prisoners are burning alive."

Brezhnev: "So why are you just standing there? Go find the marshmallows!"

OFFICIAL RUSSIAN FOUR WHEEL
DRIVE JEEP

All Russian sailors are outfitted with a rubber raft and an inflatable camel . . . in case they're marooned on a "desert" island.

* * *

The greatest naval battle in Russian history has been kept secret for years. It occurred in the summer of 1969 between the Russian flotilla and the Japanese. The Russians lost three battleships, an atomic sub, two carriers, 49 fighter planes, and 3,452 men. If you think that's bad you should see that Japanese fishing boat!

* * *

If Russia were to go to war against Iran who would win?
Russia, because their guns have bigger corks.

* * *

A king and his army had been besieging an enemy castle for weeks with no luck. A captain approached the monarch with news that he had a new secret weapon.

"What sort of weapon?" asked his kingship.

"A Russian knight, sire," replied the captain.

"And can he scale yon high wall?"

"Nay, sire."

"And can he knock down yon drawbridge?"

"Nay, sire."

"Then what, pray tell, can he do?"

"Give him a straw and he'll drink the moat!"

* * *

I don't mean to imply that Russian soldiers are clumsy and poorly trained, but every Army hospital has an express cot for recruits who shoot themselves six times or less.

* * *

Russian military experts believe that comfortable happy soldiers make the best fighters, so they instituted a new program to make the recruits' lives bearable. Trouble was, they lost 4,300 the first week. Did you ever go on a 20-mile hike carrying a waterbed?

Russian Army training film: *Deep Throat*.

* * *

Why are homosexuals with vision problems drafted into the Russian Army?

So the soldiers on the front will have "blind dates."

* * *

Why are people with impaired hearing drafted into the Russian Army?

So the enemies' pleas for mercy will fall on deaf ears.

* * *

Why are people in wheelchairs drafted into the Russian Army?

So they can be hypnotized and told that they're tanks.

* * *

What's the lowest rank in the Soviet Army?

I don't know. They're all pretty low. Come to think of it they're all pretty rank too!

Guard: "Stop right there!"

Boris: "What do you want with me?"

Guard: "Two things!"

Boris: "Well?"

Guard: "Number one, I want to ask you a few questions."

Boris: "Okay. Shoot."

Guard: "You're getting ahead of yourself. That's number two."

* * *

Russian Air Force radar: A bat on a string.

* * *

Why did the champion Russian surfer defect and seek asylum at a US naval base?

He wanted to ride the Waves.

* * *

A US naval vessel reported finding another Sargasso Sea in the Pacific. Green slime extended for miles and floated on the surface of the water. Closer investigation revealed a Russian scuba diver had been blowing his nose under water.

A Russian agent was sent out in a one-man submarine to survey the eastern coast of the US and report on the feasibility of an attack on our continent by a Soviet invasion force. He happened to surface beside the Statue of Liberty in New York Harbor and immediately radioed Moscow.

"Call off the invasion!" he warned. "You should see the size of their womenfolk!"

* * *

Russian nursery rhyme:

Rub-a-dub-dub
Three men in a tub!
A border guard saw them.
Bang! Bang! and Blub! Blub!

* * *

Why are Russian border guards like tornadoes?

They're always blowing somebody away.

* * *

During World War I a Russian division was dug into an open field. On the other side of the field the German's were firmly entrenched in a woods. Seeing that they were going to need help, the Russian general ordered his aide to send a message. The aide attached the appropriate message to a bird's leg and sent it off. It flew directly to a tree over the German lines where a sharpshooter quickly blew it to smithereens. The Russian general watched in dismay as 100 birds were sent out and all flew to tree limbs within easy range of the Kaizer's guns.

"Call quartermasters!" he screamed and ranted. "They've sent us idiot carrier pigeons!"

"Those aren't pigeons, sir," explained his aide. "We've been out of those for two years. We're using passenger woodpeckers these days."

* * *

Why didn't Russian soldiers shave during World War II?

The Germans kept blowing up their meat cleaver factories.

* * *

Is it true that Russian soldiers are really cowardly and only win battles due to overwhelming strength of numbers?

Yes! As a matter of fact, NATO's most recent plan for repelling a Soviet invasion is for three little old ladies to yell "Boo!" and scare them back across the border.

Guard #1: "I shot a heckler this morning."

Guard #2: "What happened?"

Guard #1: "He stood below my tower and yelled at me!"

Guard #2: "What did he yell?"

Guard #1: "He called me a sadistic pawn in a totalitarian scheme to unfairly control the means of production and keep the conservative masses under dictatorial domination."

Guard #2: "Wow! What does that mean?"

Guard #1: "Who knows? But the sarge was watching so I blew him away just to be safe."

* * *

The czar and his cossacks had the enemy completely surrounded. The czar immediately sent to the circus and asked for their best sword swallower.

The man arrived quickly and asked, "You called for me, sire?"

"Yes!" answered the czar, pointing to the lights of the enemy camp. "I figure they have about 4,000 swords. Can you do it?"

* * *

The Soviets have a great antimissile defense system worked out. They use their radar to track it and a peasant with a baseball mitt and a gun aimed at his head to catch it!

**OFFICIAL RUSSIAN STATE MILITARY
FUNERAL WITH HONORS!**

Machine gunfire drew a curious crowd to a scene of awful carnage. There on the street lay a smoking sleigh and eight dismembered reindeer.

As the police stuffed Santa in a body bag, one old man sobbed, "My god, man! You've murdered an institution!"

"Really?" sneered the captain of the guards. "I thought he was just another old fart roof-hopping after curfew."

Why don't Russian tanks go faster than 10 mph?

Because if they sneak up on defenseless, unsuspecting civilians in the middle of the night, they don't have to.

* * *

Why do Russian guards shoot Boy Scouts on sight?

They keep helping little old ladies across the border.

* * *

Did you hear about the Russian general who enlisted 1,000 penguins because he heard they were entering another Cold War?

* * *

Why do Russian sentries wear face masks when they have colds?

So their germs won't try to cross the border.

* * *

Why are Russian naval vessels so depressing?

Because everyone who rides one gets a real "sinking feeling."

* * *

2. From Russia with Love

Then there was the Russian nymphomaniac. She loved all the boys! So her parents sent her to a remote part of the frozen tundra where there were absolutely no males for hundreds of miles. Did she find a way? Yep! Nine months later she gave birth to a snowman.

* * *

What does a Siberian girl do before going on a date?

She defrosts her face.

* * *

Ivan: "My Uncle Petrovich was arrested for sexually molesting a cat."

Igor: "That must have shocked the family!"

Ivan: "No, he's always been a purr-vert."

How do you ruin a Russian's sex life?
Cut off his hands.

* * *

Why is playing the harmonica like kissing a Russian girl?
Because every other tooth is missing!

* * *

Then there was the Russian girl who told her boyfriend, "My heart bleeds for you!" He put a tourniquet around her neck.

* * *

Then there was the Russian who thought a "Community Chest" was when the whole village chipped in to buy one pair of falsies and everybody took turns wearing them.

* * *

A husband and wife were to be executed outside a small village in Russia. The firing squad shot the woman and hastily threw a newspaper over her face.

"It's not fair!" wept the husband. "Even today she gets the funny pages first!"

* * *

And there was the Russian witch who had a fight with her boyfriend and wanted to turn him into a toad . . . but she didn't believe in "pre-marital hex."

* * *

Boris: "My wife is just my cup of tea."
Ivan: "What do you mean?"
Boris: "Well, when I first met her she was *hot* and tempting, but I soon discovered she was just an old *bag*."

* * *

A Russian scientist had just returned from a deep sea diving expedition in search of treasure ships. He had just taken off his hat and coat when his wife walked in wearing a see-through nightie.

"Oh, yuk! Natasha!" he said covering his eyes. "I just spent two months looking at sunken chests."

Katrina: "My husband is a magician."
Ann: "Really?"
Katrina: "Yes. Since we've been married he's made over 6,000 bottles of vodka vanish, and now when he stands up his belt disappears."

Did you hear about the Russian boy who died whispering sweet things in his girl friend's ear?

He took a deep breath and inhaled an earmuff.

* * *

Then there was the mad Russian scientist who crossed a pair of overalls with two sex cells and got a pair of denim genes.

* * *

Boris: "Excuse me, miss? Are you free later tonight?"

Katrina: "No, but I'm within your budget."

* * *

Boris: "Tell me, love, when did you first realize that our marriage was in trouble?"

Natasha: "When you gave me a training bra on our first anniversary."

* * *

Then there was the Russian who thought "panty raid" was what his girl friend sprayed in her undies.

Ivan: "My wife was a flower when I married her."

Igor: "You mean she had lips like tulips, eyes like violets, and cheeks like roses?"

Ivan: "No, she had legs like roots, hair like fungus, and a complexion like a cactus!"

* * *

Ivan: "Did you see that 300-pound girl?"

Igor: "I sure did."

Ivan: "I'd sure hate to meet her in a dark alley!"

Igor: "Me too! I'd want some lights on so I wouldn't miss anything!"

* * *

Why won't Western Europeans let their daughters go out with Russians?

It costs too much to have their dresses fumigated and run them through the decontamination chamber.

* * *

Then there was the Russian whose wife left him on a rainy day. You might say he had a cold front moving in and a warm behind moving out.

How can you tell if a Russian girl is sexually aroused?

Her nose drips faster.

* * *

How can you tell if a Russian boy is sexually aroused?

His stomach growls louder.

* * *

After receiving reports that a local bar offered entertainment in the form of bottomless dancers, the police sent two of their finest to investigate. The two Russian cops got seats in the front row and scrutinized the entire show, but no arrests were made. As they were leaving, the first said, "Well, they were *almost* bottomless."

"Yeah," agreed the second. "Only those cute little toupees between their legs saved them!"

* * *

And you heard about the Russian with jock itch who made love to the girl with crabs? It was a very "rash" act.

How can you tell when a Russian girl is going out on a formal date?

She puts a silk bow in her nose hairs.

* * *

An American tourist in Moscow was looking for a place to stay. He saw a hotel with a window sign reading, "X-Movies Nightly 8 to 9 P.M." Looking at his watch and noticing he had only five minutes to catch the night's film, he hurried to the lobby, paid for the room, and ran up the stairs. He threw open the door, flipped on the TV set, and laid down on the bed. Soon the tube warmed up, the picture came into focus, and a big yellow bird said:

"And that's the letter 'X' boys and girls. Tomorrow night we will look at the letters 'Y' and 'Z'!"

* * *

Did you hear about the prince who tried a glass slipper on the foot of a Russian Cinderella?

Athlete's foot ate away his hands.

* * *

Then there was the Russian girl who kissed a frog and it turned into Prince Albert chewing tobacco.

Do Russian husbands ever get up in the middle of the night and try to sneak out on their wives?

Yes, and they're very careful not to wake them. They always take off their shoes before they fall down the stairs.

* * *

Did you hear about the Russian sex maniac who drowned?

He attacked a porcupine on a waterbed.

* * *

Igor: "I call my wife 'Poopsie'. Do you have a pet name for yours?"

Ivan: "Yes. I call her 'Iceberg'."

Igor: "Why? Is she cold?"

Ivan: "No. Three-fourths of her bulk is hidden beneath the surface of her girdle."

* * *

Never tell a Russian that somebody has stolen your heart. He'll want to dust your breasts for fingerprints.

A Russian Romeo had invited his Juliet to ride with him through a tunnel of love. Their little boat had just floated into the dark when the young lady heard a zipper come down and a belt unbuckle. The movement of her beau and the rustling of clothing made her wonder as to his intentions.

She meekly asked, "Nicolas? What are you going to do?"

"I already did," came the gruff reply. "Did you bring any toilet paper?"

* * *

Natasha: "Someday, maybe unexpectedly, you may die. Wouldn't you like to get your affairs in order?"

Boris: "Okay. In order they are: Monica, first; Katrina, second; followed by Catherine, Greta . . ."

* * *

Does the Russian man always pay for the date?

Not always. Sometimes the couple puts their chins on the table and tongue wrestle. Loser pays.

Then there was the homosexual who returned from a trip to Moscow very upset. Some Russian chess champion ran off with his "queen."

* * *

How do you recognize the mother-of-the-bride at a Russian wedding?

She's the one with the shiniest combat boots.

* * *

Russian dad: "Do you want to get in my daughter's pants?"

Russian guy: "No, sir. It's taking her long enough to get in them herself and we're late for the play already."

* * *

Two Russian snakes were crawling through a junk yard when one spied a discarded pool cue.

"Wow!" he drooled looking at the cue. "She's cute!"

"Forget it!" advised the second. "That blue lipstick looks great, but is she ever an iceberg!"

What does a Russian gourmet do when he wants to eat crab legs?

First he asks out a girl that has them.

*   *   *

Why are Russian vessels ordered to destroy any whales trying to leave their waters?

They don't want them "spouting off" in the Free World.

*   *   *

Did you hear about the Russian who believed his wife was from outer space?

He thought UFO stood for *U*gly *F*at *O*bject.

*   *   *

Why are Russian women such active lovers?

Their husbands wear spurs.

*   *   *

Did you hear about the Russian vixen who had fire in her eyes?

That's because the torch in her heart finally hit the vodka in her brain.

Why are Russian women like Indianapolis 500 drivers?

They have "fast laps."

* * *

Did you hear about the Russian woman who wanted to attract men?

Her friend told her to keep her shades up at night, so now she goes to bed with her sunglasses on her forehead.

* * *

Hugh Hefner was going to publish a *Playboy* just for Russian men, but he couldn't finish shooting the centerfold. The orangutan kept biting anyone who tried putting her in the see-through nightie.

* * *

Natasha: "Darlink! What would you say if I told you I wanted to make love in Greece?"

Boris: "I'd say you were in luck. I haven't washed in two months."

How can you tell if two old Russians are in love?

They swap teeth.

* * *

Is it true that Russian men find unshaved hairy legs attractive?

Yes. As a matter of fact a Russian was arrested the other day at the zoological gardens trying to rape a tarantula.

* * *

Igor: "I married a girl just like the girl that married dear old Dad."

Ivan: "Really?"

Igor: "Yes. She'll be 123 today."

* * *

How do Russian men get heavy dates?

They grab the first girl that comes along. They average 250 pounds.

Igor: "Right after the siege of Stalingrad, I married a girl from there."

Ivan: "Is she a good lover?"

Igor: "No, she is too weak from her ordeal."

Ivan: "Does she sew?"

Igor: "No, she's still too weak from her ordeal."

Ivan: "Does she clean house?"

Igor: "No, she's still too weak from her ordeal."

Ivan: "Then *why* did you marry her?"

Igor: "She knows 1,000 ways to cook a rat."

* * *

Foreign diplomats were invited to the Kremlin for a gala dance. One cute Ambassador's daughter was dancing with a Soviet official when he suddenly took her onto the balcony and kissed her deeply for several minutes.

"Wow!" she exclaimed as she caught her breath. "That was some kiss!"

"That's because I'm Russian!" the young man exclaimed proudly.

"No kidding?" asked the girl. "Well, do it again and this time don't rush!"

* * *

Why do Russian grooms always drive tow trucks to their weddings?

So they'll have something to help carry the bride over the threshold.

How does a Russian lady flirt?
She lifts her blouse and winks with her stretch marks.

* * *

What does it mean when a Russian girl drops her eyes?
It's time to go back to the optometrist for more glue.

* * *

Did you hear about the Russian lady who had 17 husbands? She was so fat they could all hug her at once.

* * *

Did you hear about the horribly fat Russian wife and the terribly fat Russian husband?
They died trying to make their ends meet.

* * *

Then there were the two Russian agents who fell in love and sent each other letter bombs on Valentine's Day.

Are Russian women romantic and exciting? No! They're extremely dull and boring. If you visit one in her apartment don't take flowers and champagne. Take No-doz and two toothpicks for your eyelids.

* * *

3. From Pinsk to Minsk

How can you tell if you're reading a Russian newspaper?

It doesn't have "Believe It or Not." . . . It has "Believe It or Else"!

* * *

Does Russian TV have shows like "Face the Nation"?

Sort of, only it's called "Face the Firing Squad".

* * *

Did you hear about the Russian actress who guest-starred on "Police Woman"? The producer liked her performance so much he's asked her to star in a new series. They're calling it "Police Dog."

A young Russian girl was considered beautiful in her village. Deciding that the Soviet Union offered nothing to an aspiring young model she escaped to Western Europe where she began sending her photographs to all the modeling agencies in the West. One day she received a phone call asking her to appear on the "Johnny Carson Show" and she was elated! The big night finally arrived and Johnny introduced her. She pirouetted onto the stage and floated gracefully to her seat beside the big star.

"Well," asked Carson, "how does it feel to be the winner of the Jimmy Durante Look-Alike Contest?"

* * *

It's a good thing Tom Sawyer wasn't born in Russia. Even he couldn't have tricked anybody into white washing a barbed wire fence.

* * *

The authorities had been notified that a vampire had been terrorizing the town of Omsk. The chief of police called in his best man and told him to go to the cemetery and wait.

"When the vampire returns to his grave, you take this wooden stick and drive it into his heart!"

"Couldn't somebody else do it, chief?" asked the patrolman. "You know I hate *stake-outs!*"

* * *

A toaster manufacturer had the bad luck of getting stuck with 3,000 toasters that burned the bread horribly because of a mix-up on the assembly line. He did manage to sell all of them by running an ad in a Russian paper that read:

Now you can earn up to 400 ruples a week in your own home making new fashionable flat charcoal briquets. Send $24.95 for kit and complete details.

* * *

Then there was the Russian interior decorator who painted himself into a corner in a round room.

* * *

Siberian Popsicle: A snowball on a tongue depressor.

Do the Russians embalm their dead?

Yes, and on occasion, to extract needed information, they have been known to embalm the living.

* * *

Did you hear about the Russian shoplifter who stole a grenade from an army surplus store? He decided it was too bulky to sneak out under his tunic so he decided to lighten it by putting the pin back.

* * *

Then there was the anemic Russian who took so many iron pills that when he walked out in the rain he rusted to death.

* * *

Then there was the fat overweight Russian who drank 10 bottles of vodka a day for 20 years and died trying to pass a kidney boulder.

* * *

Prez: "What are we going to do with all the Russians who have come to this country? Pen them up? Send them back? What?"

Aide: "Why not give them their own territory and let them settle there."

Prez: "That's a good idea, and I have just the place!"

Aide: "Are you thinking of giving them Georgia?"

Prez: "No! Three Mile Island!"

* * *

There's a new cookbook coming from an author in Siberia. It's titled *365 Ways to Fix Ice Cubes*.

* * *

How does a Russian pick his seat at the Bolshoi Theatre?

Well, first he pulls down his shorts . . .

* * *

Why are Russian girls like onions?

When you peel them the smell makes your eyes water.

* * *

Here lies a doc from Amderma.
A student of old terra firma.
He was close to the vent
When the volcano went
And they found his right leg down in Burma.

Dorothy, Toto, the Cowardly Lion, Tin Woodman, and Scarecrow were going down the yellow brick road when they passed a young Nikolai Lenin going in the opposite direction.

"Hi!" smiled Dorothy. "Why don't you come with us and see the Wizard?"

"Because," snarled Lenin, "I don't want to *see* the Wizard. . . . I want to *be* the Wizard!"

* * *

Build a mousetrap that not only kills the little critters but does it without ruining the flavor of the meat and all the Russians in the world will beat a path to your door.

* * *

Ivan: "Have you been to the new Lenin Memorial Health Spa?"

Igor: "Yes, but I'm not going back until they air condition the steam room!"

* * *

Russian television coverage of elections is quite sophisticated. They go out in the streets, count the bodies, and project the winner.

A Soviet barber named Jim
Decided to escape on a whim.
He spent years by his chair
Doing other folks' hair,
But now they're all combing for him!

* * *

A sick Russian gal for a cure
Was sent to recoop on the Ruhr.
She got rid of her vermin
But made love with a German
And now she's infected for sure!

* * *

Why don't they have fairy tales in Russia?
Because nobody lives "happily ever after."

* * *

How do you recognize a fashion-conscious
girl in Siberia?
She'll be wearing pierced earmuffs.

* * *

How do you recognize a Russian bird
watcher?
He's the guy with binoculars, standing on
the step ladder, looking through the transom at
the men's room.

Igor: "What this country needs is definitely *not* a 5-cent cigar!"

Ivan: "What makes you say that?"

Igor: "I just sat next to a guy smoking a 5-cent cigar!"

* * *

P.T. Barnum was wrong. Since the Russian population explosion there's now a sucker born every 35 seconds.

* * *

Why don't Russian kids like M & Ms?
They're too hard to peel.

* * *

Did you hear about the Russian star gazer?
They caught him peeping in Bea Arthur's window.

* * *

The Russians gave up on ever landing on the Moon. They figured it would cost $1.8 billion to plant their flag there and $300 billion for trips back and forth to water it.

Is it true that Russians are born cowards?
I don't know . . . but their noses are always running.

* * *

Here lies a pilot named Nyet
Who bailed out over Tibet.
An angry young Yeti
Tore his chute to confetti
And they're searching for parts of him yet.

* * *

A large airline company in the United States had been told by the government that it needed to hire at least one token Russian. One day the company's chief executive was visiting the airport and asked the personnel director: "Did you find a job for that idiot Russian?"

"I sure did!" beamed the personnel man. "I put him on maintenance and clean-up."

"You what?" yelled the president. "You imbecile! That Russian doesn't know anything about airplanes!"

"Relax, sir. I gave him a rug beater and told him to take care of any flying carpets that happen to come in."

A Russian explorer with a completely bald head had been captured by African cannibals. He waited nervously for the inevitable end he knew would come. Soon a big black ferocious-looking cannibal entered the hut.

"A-a-are y-you the c-c-cook?" stammered the Russian.

"No, me no cook."

"Phew!" sighed the prisoner as he wiped his bald pate.

"Me tattoo expert," said the native as he unsheathed a huge knife. "And you is going to be chief's new globe!"

* * *

Why do Russian parents lie, cheat, and steal in front of their kids?

They want to set a good example.

* * *

Then there was the shrewd American tourist who took a box of stale Cheerios to a beach in Russia and sold them at $2 per Cheerio. He told the bathers they were condensed, freeze-dried innertubes.

* * *

Why was the Russian couple expelled from Long John Silver's Seafood Shoppe?

They ordered a raw carp and two straws.

How can you recognize a Russian guy in the men's room?

He's the hairy one reading the dirty sayings on the wall, applauding, and yelling "Author! Author!"

* * *

In Russia a person who dies of a shotgun wound is said to have "died of natural causes."

* * *

Russians don't spend money on Copper Tone or Sea & Ski. They just yell "This country stinks!" and the government tans their hide free.

* * *

In Russia you're considered antisocial if you don't have at least one bullet hole in your body.

* * *

Why do Russian parents start giving their kids vodka at an early age?

So they can start learning to belch the national anthem.

Siberian postcard: "Wish I wasn't here!"

* * *

Does the average Russian have any religious views?

No, but they have some great color slides of Siberia.

* * *

Do Russians make good public speakers?

No, they stutter. Ask 'em what country they're from and they'll say "Duh! C-C-C-P!"

* * *

After the number of starvation deaths during the sieges of Stalingrad and Leningrad, the Russians are making sure it won't happen again. Their top scientists have developed a product to make existing food supplies last longer. It's called Rat Extender.

* * *

Why are so many Russian urban commuters injured everyday?

Their subway trains have ejection seats.

How do Russian mothers diaper their babies?

With a 20-gallon trash bag and a pair of suspenders.

* * *

How do Russians punctuate most sentences?
They use quotation Marx.

* * *

Then there was the Russian scientist who came up with jumper cables for fireflies.

* * *

Then there was the Russian torturer who always kept a box of Tide on hand so he could get his subjects to *come clean.*

* * *

Did you hear about the Russian torturer?
His favorite candy was licorice *whips.* His stockbroker was Merrill *Lynch.* His favorite card game was *Rack*-o.

Then there was the Russian scholar who put two barbells on top of his dictionary. He wanted to "build-up" his vocabulary.

*　*　*

Then there was the Russian astronaut who was shot for going to the Miss Universe pageant to observe the heavenly bodies.

*　*　*

Why are Russian women among the most fertile in the world?

They're usually covered with 2 inches of rich topsoil.

*　*　*

Beware if a Russian gentleman throws his cloak over a mud puddle. It probably has a dagger in it.

*　*　*

Is it true that Russian fishermen stand up in canoes and wee-wee over the side?

Only into a passing canoe.

Then there was the Russian dignitary who took his pet elephant to the hotel. The bellboy hemorrhaged trying to get the trunk upstairs.

* * *

Then there was the Russian who spent five hours dangling a worm and hook inside his radio trying to catch a "channel catfish."

* * *

Did you hear about how the Russian oil driller died?

A trucker caught him attacking his rig with a Black and Decker.

* * *

Then there was the mad Russian scientist who crossed a guy who hated salesmen with a magician and got a brute who saws Avon ladies in half.

* * *

And the mad Russian scientist who crossed a guy from Prague with an Indian rubber man and got a check that bounced.

Igor: "I had one-man show for my latest oil paintings!"

Ivan: "That's good!"

Igor: "It was big honor, but I am quitting oil painting now."

Ivan: "Why?"

Igor: "Government has cut off my ration of 10-W-40!"

* * *

Then there was the Russian who wanted to be an Indian so he bought a "bow" tie and an "Arrow" shirt.

* * *

Ivan: "Did you sell any of your oil paintings during the show?"

Igor: "No. Government art critic give me bad write up. But I got even.

Ivan: "What did you do?"

Igor: "I poisoned his seeing-eye dog."

* * *

Hollywood once employed a Russian as a prompter. He sat offstage in a banana tree and read Cheeta her lines.

Igor: "Government is hanging one of my oil paintings in state museum."

Ivan: "That is big honor . . . being framed framed by the state.

Igor: "Not really. Forty thousand Siberian prisoners can claim same thing."

* * *

Igor: "Kremlin be asking me to do paintings for them."

Ivan: "Igor originals?"

Igor: "Kind of. I go to Siberia to do a "Blue Boy," to torture chamber to do "Moaning Lisa," and to death row to do "Last Supper."

* * *

Did you hear about the Russian who put his shoes on the wrong feet? The guy actually ran away in them and didn't bring them back!

* * *

Did you hear about the Russian mad scientist who crossed a headhunter with a missile and got a shrunken warhead?

And you heard about the two Russian geologists who died trying to eat their way to the earth's *core*?

* * *

Then there was the slick trader who peeled 1,000,000 bananas and sold them to a Russian fertilizer plant as rare vitamin-enriched albino dog poop.

* * *

Then the crafty slick trader sold the Moscow museum two coconuts. At $5,000 each. He told them they were petrified mammoth testicles.

* * *

A Russian farmer had just planted a huge crop of corn, and fearing the Russian crows would eat it, stuck a giant scarecrow in the field. He awoke next morning to find the crows tearing the thing to bits, screeching and throwing straw in every direction. This went on for weeks. Everyday the farmer built a new scarecrow and every day the birds destroyed it.

Soon the corn began to grow and the attacks diminished. Seeing a wary crow in a nearby tree the farmer asked:

"What's the matter? Did you birds finally give up?"

"Heck, no!" exclaimed the crow. "We're afraid of corn!"

* * *

Ivan be nimble,
Ivan be quick,
Ivan jump over the dynamite stick.
Ivan not fast enough.
Dynamite blow!
Now Ivan have to sit down when he go.

* * *

Ivan, Ivan, sat on a wall.
Ivan, Ivan, had a great fall.
All the king's horsemen
Thought he was dead.
But lucky for Ivan
He lit on his head!

* * *

Are Russians afraid of little green men from Mars?

No, they're more worried about the little yellow ones from Peking.

Then there was the Russian lady who bought a wig two sizes too small. She flew to Africa to get her head shrunk.

* * *

Then there was the Russian cowboy who always slept in a mud hole when out on the prairie. He preferred a water-bed!

* * *

Hollywood is going to do a new epic movie called *Flea Circus* starring actual fleas. It'll be a low-budget film. All they have to do is hire one Russian and he'll provide them with a cast of thousands.

* * *

Then there was the Russian who went into "hog farming," but his pigs all died. He planted them too deep.

* * *

I suppose you heard about the tornadoes that swept through Moscow causing an estimated $5,000,000,000 in improvements.

Did you hear about the Russian who invested in a birddog to earn a little extra money?

He already has advance orders for 300 dozen eggs.

* * *

Do they have talent shows in Russia?

Yes, they much resemble our American "Gong Show" . . . if you can picture Rex Reed and J. P. Morgan with machine guns.

* * *

Why does the Russian Bible have only 65 books instead of 66?

Because they're Ruth-less

* * *

What does the local madam do when the Russian troops come to town?

She puts lipstick on the pigs.

* * *

Russian grain mill: A pinwheel in a bowl of Wheaties.

A Russian family had sat down to enjoy a plate full of Grandma's hot, freshly baked cookies. Suddenly they noticed Grandma wasn't eating.

"Hey, Grandma! Why aren't you eating?"

"Can't."

"How come?"

"No false teeth."

"Where are they."

"Soaking in soapy water."

"Why?"

"I used them for a cookie cutter!"

* * *

How do you get a Russian kid to eat his spaghetti-o's?

Tell him they're barbecued belly buttons.

* * *

Why are Russian tanks always breaking down?

They wind the rubber bands too tight.

* * *

They're doing a new James Bond film in Russia about a Soviet proctologist. It's called *Brown Finger*.

Russian money clip: Tab from aluminum beer can.

* * *

Siberian toilet paper: Ice pick.

* * *

Then there were the two Russian snakes who happened upon a lawn sprinkler.

"Gee, that's a shame!" said the first.

"Sure is!" agreed the second. "Worst case of diarrhea I've ever seen!"

* * *

How do old Russian women pass the time of day?

They talk to artificial plants.

* * *

Did you hear about the Russian homosexual who's trying to build a time machine so he can live in the "gay nineties?"

* * *

Then there was the Russian piano player who flunked typing class. She kept hitting chords.

Is it really cold in Siberia?

Yeah, it's so cold their doormats say "W-w-wel-c-come!"

* * *

The Russians are using the wheat we sold them to make a sugar-coated breakfast cereal. . . . They're calling it "Tricks."

* * *

An Indiana farmer, feeling sorry for a blind Russian immigrant agreed to rent him a room in his house for a modest price. One day the farmer found the Russian sitting on the side of the well with his pants down and his behind over the edge.

"I can put up with this big toilet," said the blind Ruskie as he pointed over his shoulder at the outhouse. "But you'll have to do something about that awful tasting water in that well."

* * *

Actually there were three Noahs. The one we read about in the Bible who repopulated the earth. The Russian one who gunned down the animals as they tried to leave the ark. And the Jewish one who looked around the ark after the animals left, invested in a second-hand shovel, and made it big in the fertilizer business.

Why don't Russians burn to death in their sleep during house fires?

They have too many wet dreams.

* * *

Did you hear about the little Russian kid who bled to death during toilet training?

Everytime he hit the bullseye he put a notch in his "gun."

* * *

Why did the dead Russian take his bathing suit to hell?

He heard they had a heated pool.

* * *

How do you recognize the Russian among a group of pirates?

He's the one with two eye patches, two peg legs, and two hooks instead of hands.

* * *

What do you call a garbage can in Moscow?
The souvenir shop.

Why isn't color TV popular in the Soviet Union?

It's rather boring when all the programs are "red."

* * *

Did you hear about the Russian hockey team?

They drowned during spring training.

* * *

Why do Russian women wear bright red bikinis when they're sunbathing in Siberia?

So you can tell them from woolly mammoths.

* * *

Russian bullet-proof vest: Two pounds of starch and an undershirt.

* * *

How does a Russian put up wallpaper?
With bandaids.

OFFICIAL RUSSIAN BOWLING BALL

Did you hear about the New York businessman who made the mistake of hiring a Russian secretary? He had to send her to a special school for six months of intensive training. But it worked! She finally learned how to hold a pencil!

* * *

What should you do if a Russian offers you a chair?

Check the room for a plug and wall switch.

* * *

Then there was the Russian TV weatherman who said, "I think it's a nice day out there, but it's so foggy I can't tell."

* * *

Then there was the Russian superman who got so high on LSD he thought he *couldn't* fly.

* * *

Then there was the Russian hunter who went out to bag a lion . . . armed with a grocery sack and a twist tie.

How many Russians does it take to move a piano?

Sixty. One to aim it and 59 to go outside and tilt the house.

*   *   *

And there was the Russian who thought a "flash attachment" was what dirty old men kept hidden under their trenchcoats.

*   *   *

How did they get phone service in the Soviet Union?

Ma Bell had a miscarriage.

*   *   *

Why is an ancient castle door like an old Russian woman?

They both have aged knockers.

*   *   *

Why do Russians eat banana splits very slowly?

They don't always get all the tarantula bones out of them.

Then there was the mad Russian scientist who crossed a pair of underwear with a large African antelope and got a gnu's brief.

*   *   *

Why don't Russians bite their tongues?
They never close their mouths.

*   *   *

Why do Russian office workers have terry cloth desk blotters?
They drool a lot.

*   *   *

They did away with the law in the Soviet Union that all motorcyclists must wear helmets. The pedestrians they hit died anyway.

*   *   *

When does a Russian lady take off her bra?
When her lice want to ski jump.

*   *   *

How can you tell the difference between a Mexican and a Russian at a festival dance?

The Mexican's the one dancing around the brim of the sombrero. The Russian's the guy wearing the sombrero and bleeding from both ears.

*　*　*

Frank and Jesse James had a Russian sidekick for awhile. Jesse carried the six shooter. Frank carried the bags of loot. The Russian carried a shovel and cleaned up after the getaway horses.

*　*　*

Robin Hood had a Russian immigrant in his band of merry men. He only lasted one season. Friar Tuck used him for a camp stool.

*　*　*

Then there was the Russian witch who captured Hansel and Gretel. The kids escaped. Her cage had candy bars.

*　*　*

How does a Russian artist paint sky in his landscapes?
With an *air*brush.

When does a Russian jump in the bathtub?
When his pet body lice want to go to the beach.

*   *   *

When does a Russian shave?
When his pet lice want their lawn mowed.

*   *   *

Many ships of many nations had crashed on the rocks near the northern coast of the Soviet Union. In spite of a tall lighthouse, hundreds of vessels were lost yearly. Finally a UN commission was sent to the lighthouse to find out what was wrong. They found a crusty old Russian in charge.

"Is this your lighthouse?" asked one investigator.

"Yes," replied the keeper.

"Does it have a light?"

"Yes."

"Does the light work?"

"Yes."

"Then why don't you use it?"

"I do use it."

"What for?"

"I use it to watch shipwrecks at night."

OFFICIAL RUSSIAN EYE CHART

Why did the Russian fill his glass with sand?
He wanted an extra dry martini.

* * *

Then there was the Russian lady who took her bath towel and scrub brush to a bridal shower.

* * *

Why are Russians such great weight lifters?
Because their family tree contains so many dumbbells.

* * *

Did you hear about the Russian race car driver who ran into the wall seventy-two times in one day?
Somebody finally pointed him toward the door and he walked out of the men's room.

* * *

Then there was the Russian who thought a "maidenhead" was where virgins went to the bathroom.

Ivan: "Well at age 38 I finally got up enough courage to solo."

Igor: "Really? How was it?"

Ivan: "When I pulled back on that stick and let fly it was the greatest feeling in the world."

Igor: "It is a great accomplishment to fly a plane."

Ivan: "Who flew a plane? I went to the toilet by myself."

* * *

Are Russian girls pretty?
Yeah! Pretty awful!

* * *

How do you recognize a Russian at a birthday party?
He's the hairy one with the 50-caliber noisemaker.

* * *

What is the shortest book in Russia?
The Tourist's Guide to Unbombed Buildings in Stalingrad.

The Russians have designed a new toilet. When you pull the handle, it covers you with confetti and plays Auld Lang Syne. It's called a "Party Pooper!"

*   *   *

Did you hear about the Russian kangaroo who died from a ruptured pouch? She opened a day care center for kids.

*   *   *

A terrible flood had put two Russian farmers on top of their house to escape the rising waters. One was terribly depressed. The other, being more optimistic said, "Try looking at the bright side, comrade. The crops aren't thirsty anymore!"

*   *   *

Then there were the two Russians who crawled 20 miles across the desert and finally came to a water hole. What could they do? They had to crawl back 20 miles to get their fishing poles.

OFFICIAL
RUSSIAN
CHARM
BRACELET

Did you know that if you took all the attractive intelligent people in Russia and laid them end to end, they'd both have back-aches by morning?

* * *

How does a Russian actor break into show business?

He attacks the stage door with a crowbar.

* * *

Do Russian ladies like to "squeeze the Charmin?"

Yes, especially after they've used it.

* * *

Do Russians pick their noses?

No, they have to settle with the one they're born with, like everybody else.

* * *

How does a Russian housewife do the dishes?

She piles them in the toilet and flushes.

Have they ever had a strike in the Soviet Union?

Naw! They're terrible bowlers!

* * *

Are Russian dogs stupid?

Yes, they walk backwards and wag their heads.

* * *

How many inches of rainfall during a typical Russian spring?

Who knows? Their rain gauges keep floating away.

* * *

Is it true that the Soviet Union contains 8,650,000 square miles?

Yes, and it contains 250,000,000 square people.

* * *

Did you hear about the Russian wolfhound who went to obedience school? On show-and-tell day he took a mailman's leg.

Then there was the Russian who demanded his money back from the pet store. He plugged in his electric eel and it melted.

* * *

Hollywood is making a new movie to follow *Flipper* and *Son of Flipper*. It will star a Russian actor and will be called *Afterbirth of Flipper*.

* * *

Russian deodorant block: Limburger cheese.

* * *

What is the speed limit in Russia?
Each party member is allowed to "shoot-up" once a day.

* * *

Why won't a rabbi take a Russian out to dinner?
Because they eat like pigs.

Ivan: "My cousin is no longer a symphony conductor."

Igor: "What happened?"

Ivan: "The state asked him to conduct the orchestra at the Veterans Hospital in Moscow for the permanently disabled, and after the performance they fired him."

Igor: "Didn't the musicians play well?"

Ivan: "Yes, but *Cripple Creek* was a poor choice of music."

* * *

Why did the Russian slaughter 4,000 hogs?

He was pearl-diving among the Rocky Mountain oysters.

* * *

Did you hear about the Russian window washer who died? He fell behind in his work.

* * *

Russian formal dance: Foul ball.

* * *

Russian cherry cobbler: A virgin shoe repairman.

"I guess this means they'll cancel the croquet tournament at the park!"

Then there was the Siberian eskimo who was depressed. There was such a fuel shortage that the government closed the dog food stores on weekends.

* * *

Why does every Russian lady's beauty kit contain a plumber's friend suction tool?

So they can clean out their pores.

* * *

Russians have a dangerous sport that makes Niagara Falls' daredevils look like amateurs. They flush themselves down the toilet in a barrel.

* * *

Why is it compulsory that all Russian ladies learn to swim?

Because 4 out of 10 of them will eventually become tugboats.

* * *

Is it true that Russians relieve themselves in church?

Yes. That's why you call them Pughs.

There there were two Russians arrested for cruelty to animals. They were caught breaking the wish-bone before the chicken died.

* * *

Are Russians too dumb to get in out of the rain?

No, but they usually get *in* at the car wash.

* * *

Do Russian marksmen hit the bulls-eye often?

As a matter of fact, they shoot low. Which is the reason the calf population is falling off drastically.

* * *

How does a Russian stop foot odor?

He puts a land mine in each shoe.

* * *

Then there was the Russian weakling who sent for the Charles Atlas Body Building Course after he went to the beach and a 2-gram fly kicked sand in his face.

Does a Russian's underwear pose a laundry problem?

Only if he can't find his sand-blaster.

* * *

In the third century BC a Russian discovered the noose and invented death by hanging. Four hundred years later, a Hun said, "What if we put it around their necks instead of their ankles?"

* * *

How did the Mona Lisa get that wonderful smile?

You can thank a Russian flasher.

* * *

Did you hear about the Russian who got on a Boeing 747? It taxied about 50 feet before he fell off.

* * *

What is the biggest bomb that Russia has ever had?

That's hard to say. All of their plays are pretty awful.

Do Russians have "horse sense?"
I don't know, but they love sugar cubes!

* * *

Do the Russians have any good high jumpers?
Naw! Even their sober ones are bad.

* * *

Peter: "My wife's been bugging me for years to get her indoor plumbing!"
Boris: "So? Did you do it?"
Peter: "Sure. I cut a hole in the living room floor and brought the catalogues and corn cobs inside.

* * *

How many seats in a Russian stadium?
How should I know? Count the cheeks and divide by two!

* * *

Do Russian teenagers ever "streak?"
No, but if you run over them in a truck they'll smear!

What should you take with you to a Russian theatre?

A bag of popcorn, a chocolate bar, and a sani-cover for the seat.

*   *   *

Boris: "My wife is lifting weights to reduce."

Ivan: "How's it working?"

Boris: "Pretty good. The weights are getting thinner."

*   *   *

Is there such a thing as a Russian "pool shark?"

Yes. One ate three people yesterday at the YMCA.

*   *   *

Then there was the mad Russian scientist who crossed a steno pad with a circus and got a three-ring binder that smells like a menagerie.

*   *   *

Russian Frisbee: Manhole cover.

Boris: "A policeman was stabbed on my street yesterday and he died."

Ivan: "Yeah, but he'll rise again."

Boris: "How do you know?"

Ivan: "Most scum does."

* * *

Two Russian skiers had been half-buried by an avalanche when a St. Bernard suddenly appeared with a flask of vodka around his neck.

"Look!" exclaimed the first Russian. "It's man's best friend!"

"So it is!" said the second. "And he has a dog with him!"

* * *

Why don't they have any A & W Root Beer stands in Russia?

The trays won't hang on the tanks.

* * *

Since they can't beat the US by scoring more goals, the Soviet Hockey Team is trying to get a new event entered in the next Winter Olympics: "Penalty box cramming."

It's a good thing the Russians don't have a free enterprise system. They'd be hard up for salesmen. It's true! They're horrible sales getters. I once saw one fail to sell fresh manure to a starving fly!

* * *

The price of manure has dropped drastically on the world market. Some idiot ran over a Russian and discovered the mother lode.

* * *

Then there was the famous Russian Diver who dove 6 inches off of a glass of water onto a wooden platform.

* * *

Can fortune tellers read a Russian's mind? Yes, but they usually wait for the movie.

* * *

Are Russians prone to accidents? No, most of them have 'em standing up.

OFFICIAL RUSSIAN ELECTRIC SWEEPER

Why do native-born Russians make great train engineers?

Because their brains are HO scale.

* * *

Do you know how to turn a Russian girl's head?

Grab it by both ears and twist!

* * *

Why hasn't Russia's greatest architect built any new buildings lately?

Somebody stole his Tinker toys!

* * *

Why aren't there any Chinese restaurants in Russia?

Because the government insists on censoring their fortune cookies.

* * *

How many Russians does it take to wash a car?

Forty. One to wipe and thirty-nine to spit.

Then there was the Russian who thought a cocktail party was an orgy at a nudist colony.

* * *

Do they have a problem with women's liberation in Russia?

Yes. Only yesterday two old ladies made a run for the border.

* * *

Sign in Russian cafe window:
No shoes, no shirt, no service!
No bra, no panties, we'll talk about it.

* * *

Then there was the traveling salesman who stopped at a Russian immigrant's farmhouse and asked if he could sleep with the oldest daughter. He was told there were already a sheep, two bulls, a stallion, and a rooster ahead of him.

* * *

And you heard about the Russian who took a bag of bread crumbs to the parking garage so he could feed the meters.

Do Russian interrogators always get the naked truth?

No. Once in awhile they torture people with their clothes on.

* * *

Do Russian women throw rolling pins at their husbands?

Yes, and they're almost always followed by a bouncing grenade.

* * *

Do they have a race problem in Russia?

Yes, their drivers, jockeys, and runners always finish last.

* * *

Then there was the Russian who wanted to commit suicide but couldn't decide whether to electrocute himself or take sleeping pills. So he compromised . . . he took four flashlight batteries and swallowed them with a glass of water.

Then there was the Russian who went to buy a car. The salesman asked: "Did you want a straight stick, sir?"

"Why?" asked the Russian. "Are crooked ones cheaper?"

* * *

And you heard about the Russian who ate a copy of their constitution and rushed to the bathroom to "pass a new law."

* * *

Ivan, Ivan! What a kid!
Think of all the sins he did.
A hundred thousand wrongs at least.
I guess he'll never be a priest.

* * *

A Russian Snow White asked her mirror:
"Are there any drugs hid near?"
The mirror thought hard then answered "Nope!"
"Ivan is the only *dope*."

Then there was the Russian who thought the Boston Marathon was the only place you could buy gas in Massachusetts.

* * *

Do Russians *make* good pets?
Never leave a Russian man alone in a room with any kind of pet!

* * *

Then there was the Russian lion tamer who was fired from the circus. He was good with cats and the crowd loved him but he kept putting his head in the wrong end.

* * *

How many Russians does it take to make a barber shop quartet?
Ten. Four to sing the parts and six to pump the chair that gooses the soprano so he can hit the high notes.

* * *

What's the first thing a Russian lady does after giving birth to a baby?
She hangs a sign on her stomach: Womb for rent!

How can you recognize a Russian in a Western saloon?

He's the guy chug-a-lugging the spittoon.

*   *   *

How does a Russian make wine in a hurry?

He fills his mouth with grapes and lets three fat peasants stomp on his face.

*   *   *

Are there any flat-chested Russian women?

Yes. Two thousand of them earned $25 a day playing mud flaps in the Soviet version of *Convoy*.

*   *   *

What is the fanciest finishing school for Russian girls?

The Sam Peckinpah Institute for Etiquette.

*   *   *

Are Russian men sharp dressers?

Are you kidding? With all those concealed knives and daggers they have to be.

What should you take with you on a picnic in a Moscow park?
Vulture repellent.

* * *

Is Russian food really greasy?
I'll say! When you order a sandwich they have to staple on the bread.

* * *

Russian breath freshener: Lysol!

* * *

If a Russian starts a job will he stick to it?
Only if it comes in contact with his skin.

* * *

What does St. Peter do when a Russian arrives in heaven?
He assigns them to a mushroom cloud.

* * *

Why are Russian waiting rooms always full of water?
Because most of them couldn't wait.

OFFICIAL RUSSIAN DICE

How do Russians christen their babies?
They break a bottle of vodka on their heads.

* * *

Ivan bought an army jeep.
He made it go real fast . . . the creep!
He aims it well and that's a shame
Cause children are his only game!

* * *

Ivan bought a piece of rope.
Injected it with hard-line dope.
He built a gallows to the sky
And now his friends are hanging *high*.

* * *

Ivan bought a surplus Tank
And drove it to a nearby bank.
He got the cash. It wasn't hard.
He used his "Tank-Americard."

* * *

Ivan has a torture rack
To cure the worst insomniac.
He simply pulls the little lever
And puts the guy to sleep forever.

Ivan has a brand-new gun.
He bought it just to use for fun.
He shows his friends and says "Surprise!"
And shoots them right between the eyes.

* * *

Ivan has a guillotine.
The blade is steel and very keen.
The ladies think he's cute and dear.
They lose their heads when Ivan's near.

* * *

Ivan bought some dynamite.
And ran an ad: "Get high tonight!"
Look him up and you will find
This dude can really "blow your mind!"

* * *

Ivan bought a pair of pliers.
He uses them to question liars.
If they refuse to tell the truth.
He simply pulls another tooth.

* * *

Ivan with a bayonet
Stabbed his parents and his pet.
Poked his kid and sliced his wife.
He's been a "cut-up" all his life.

111

Ivan took a live grenade
And hid it in the lemonade.
He likes to joke. He's such a smartie!
He'll make a blast of any party.

* * *

What's the difference between Washington and Lenin?
Washington chopped down cherry trees. Lenin mowed down people.

* * *

Then there was the Russian who thought an illegal alien was a Martian born out of wedlock.

* * *

The Russian city of Irkutsk is mass producing a new van for the world market. It has crummy gas mileage, looks awful, and is a mechanical nightmare. It's called: "I. Van the Terrible."

* * *

A Russian and his wife were out driving when a truck crossed the center line and hit them head on. The truck driver crawled from his wrecked vehicle and managed to inch over to the demolished car. There he saw the Russian calmly rolling a cigarette while his wife bled horribly.

"Hey!" groaned the injured trucker. "Couldn't you at least try a tourniquet or something?"

"I've tried before," answered the unconcerned hubby. "But when it's her time of the month, it's her time of the month."

* * *

Once upon a time there was a Russian who immigrated to South Carolina in the days before the Civil War. Being industrious and imaginative, he soon owned one of the biggest tobacco plantations in the state. He was known around the area as being very, very tight with his cash, so his wife was amazed when he threw down the evening paper and shouted:

"Get a big bag of money and let's go!"

"Where?" asked his surprised spouse.

"To Charleston," was the reply. "The paper says they're having a huge white sale at the dry goods store."

"You want to take advantage of a white sale?" she asked.

"Certainly," he responded. "I've never owned a white before, but its cheaper than bleaching the slaves."

Cinderella waited in anticipation for the arrival of her Fairy Godmother. Finally there came a knock at the door, and she opened it to find a hairy cossack.

"You're not my Godmother!" exclaimed Cindy.

"All the Godmothers got other engagements tonight," explained the Russian. "So you'll have to settle for a plain old 'Fairy'!"

* * *

Why do Russians wear spurs on their prom shoes?

They like plenty of room when they dance.

* * *

Do Russians have bad breath?

Well, let's put it this way, if one of them throws you a kiss you can knock it out of the air.

* * *

Igor: "My wife is a terrible cook!"

Ivan: "Come now. She can't be that bad."

Igor: "Oh yeah? Where do you think the Reverend James Jones got his Kool-aid recipe?"

What is a Russian Soft Drink?
A cotton ball soaked in vodka.

* * *

Totsky: "Can I go out and play?"
Momsky: "Not until you practice your lying lesson."

* * *

Tourist: "How's the fishing?"
Russian: "It be fine. See? I catch 14 big ones."
Tourist: "Those are big! What kind of line are you using?"
Russian: "Same one I always use . . . 'Here, Fishy, Fishy'!"

* * *

A Russian diplomat was buying his groceries on his first trip to a US supermarket. Seeing that he was obviously confused, the store manager asked if he could help.

"Yes, please," answered the exasperated Soviet. "I be finding extra-crispy, extra-crunchy, extra-meaty, extra-zesty. Don't you have anything extra-cheap?"

Did you hear about the Russian surfer who drowned?

He spurred his rubber horsie and it sank.

*   *   *

What does a Russian scientist do when his terribly expensive, very elaborate, extremely sophisticated electronic computer breaks down?

He pounds on the top.

*   *   *

How does a Russian bowler get "300?"

He adds up the scores of his last 152 games.

*   *   *

Why do so many nudists move to Russia?

Because of the "raw" weather.

*   *   *

Did you hear about the starving Russian?

He was so hungry that he butchered, cured, and ate his kid's piggy bank.

Then there was the Russian in New York who opened an office on an escalator so his business would go up.

* * *

Russian traffic sign: "Watch for falling re-gimes."

* * *

Then there was the Russian who heard it was cheaper to cook with gas so he went home, farted into a Bic lighter, and blew his brains out.

* * *

How can you tell if a Russian sends you a birthday present?
It'll come in red paper with a barb-wire bow.

* * *

How are Russian athletes able to throw the discus so far?
They imagine it's a dishful of their wife's cooking.

How do you recognize a Russian cashier in a restaurant?

He's the bleeding dummy with the spindle through his hand.

A team of two scientists, one American the other Russian, were diving in the Pacific. Suddenly a huge shark appeared and swallowed the Soviet diver in one gulp.

The American scientist screamed: "Oh, my God! A maneater!"

"Oh, my God!" retched the shark. "Not anymore!"

* * *

How does a Russian teenager soup-up his hot rod?

He washes it in Chicken Noodle-Os.

* * *

Why don't Russian women wear bikini bathing suits?

It's too much of a hassle shaving their stomachs.

* * *

How can you recognize a Russian lady at the laundromat?

She's the one shaking the hair out of her bra.

How can you recognize a Russian lady at the fruit stand?

She's the one with the tape measure checking the worms to be sure she's getting her money's worth.

* * *

How do you recognize a Russian lady at the parking garage?

She's the one trying to parallel park the half-track.

* * *

A fat Russian entered an American men's store. Seeing the proprietor he said, "I want real fashion plate man's suit, comrade."

The owner found the largest suit he had, a 46-long gray pinstripe, but it was still several sizes too small. After a few grunts and tugs he finally managed to get it on the hefty Russian.

"Is this real fashion plate man's suit?" asked the visitor.

"Indeed it is, sir!"

"It is latest color?"

"Yes, and the newest style."

"Is it split in the back?"

"No," pondered the seller, "but wear it a few times and it will be."

How do you recognize a Russian lady at a Halloween party?

She's the only one whose face isn't false.

* * *

Eskimo: "What happened to the roof of the igloo?"

Eskimae: "It's my fault, dear. You were right. It was bad luck opening an umbrella in the house."

* * *

Are Russian mosquitoes very big?

Huge! One buzzed an airport near Iran and the control tower gave it clearance to land.

* * *

If you own a genuine photograph of a real Russian, be sure and hang on to it. False-face manufacturers pay big money for blue-prints.

* * *

A tourist in Moscow had heard awful stories that even the finest restaurants in the city served dog meat on occasion. The first question he asked his waiter was: "Do you serve dog meat here?"

The waiter looked horrified. "Oh, no! Never, comrade!"

"Okay then," said the American. "I'll have a steak."

The meal was quite satisfactory, but in the middle of the night he woke up with a terrible stomachache that nothing could cure. He stormed into the restaurant next day, found his waiter, and spun him around. "I thought you didn't serve dog meat here!" he said angrily.

"But comrade! I be telling you only truth!"

"Then how come I'm constipated?"

"What means this 'constipated'?"

"I can't go to the toilet. Nothing happens!"

The waiter thought for awhile then asked, "Have you tried kicking yourself in the stomach and telling it to 'Giddy-up, Go'?"

* * *

Nick: "How'd you like Russia?"

Dick: "I didn't."

Nick: "Didn't you go to that topless restaurant I told you about?"

Dick: "Yeah, I went."

Nick: "And did they have a topless waitress?"

Dick: "Yeah, they had one."

Nick: "So? Was she built?"

Dick: "Who knows? There was a cloud of flies around her so thick I couldn't see anything."

Did you hear about the Russian who had a TV dinner?

He choked on the picture tube.

* * *

How does a Russian install a seatbelt?

He sits on a vodka bottle.

* * *

Can a Russian beat an egg?

Only if he cheats.

* * *

Then there was the little German boy who found some dog poop in the front yard and took it into his mother.

"Where did you find that?" exclaimed the horrified parent.

"Under the tree in the front yard," said the lad.

"You put it back this instant!" ordered his mother. "If the Russian lady comes back and finds you've been fooling in her nest she's liable to abandon it."

OFFICIAL
RUSSIAN
HAMBURGER
PRESS

Then there was the jeweler who tried to pierce a Russian's ears and died in an avalanche of earwax.

* * *

Great Russian scientific discovery: "When you dip red litmus paper into an acid solution it gets wet."

* * *

Ivan: "Cousin Peter is an interrogator for the police and he tortures people to music."
Igor: "What's his favorite song?"
Ivan: "Scars and Stripes Forever."

* * *

The Soviet government is constantly trying the latest in scientific discoveries to get the most out of their farm production. This sounds fine in theory, but did you ever try biting into a chicken breast full of silicone?

* * *

Then there was the Russian "self-made man" who started out "in the gutter," and after 30 years of hard work and shrewd investments he ended up on the sidewalk.

126

Did you hear about the Russian who tried to drive a truck?

Broke his golf club to smithereens!

*   *   *

Russian night club: A baseball bat with a candle on one end.

*   *   *

Natasha: "Did you enjoy your tour of Scandinavia?"

Katrina: "Oh, yes. It was delightful."

Natasha: "Did you see any royalty?"

Katrina: "Well, I almost did."

Natrina: "Almost?"

Katrina: "Yes. Someone yelled 'Here comes Baron Olaf himself,' so I closed my modest little eyes."

*   *   *

Is it true that Russian men are known child molesters?

Yes. Never take your baby out in Moscow in a see-through bib.

*   *   *

The Russians have decided to compete for the world junk merchandise market. They're marking all their exports: Made Real Close to Japan.

Why did the Russian buy three thousand dead fish?

So his wife could make him a "herring-bone" suit.

* * *

In the days of the old West an immigrant Russian farmer was minding his own business. He was sitting on high ground looking over his spread when two desperadoes rode into the valley below, jumped off their mounts, urinated on a cactus, and galloped off. Soon the sheriff and his posse came along, and, seeing the old Russian, they asked:

"Did you see two men ride this way?"

"Yes."

"Which way did they go?"

"Standing up."

* * *

You heard about the Russian who managed to sneak up during a concert and get a close-up photo of Dolly Parton's chest? There wasn't a drug store big enough to develop the prints.

* * *

Why can't Russian women learn to disco? When they dip they stick to the floor.

How can you recognize a Russian parachutist?

He's the one holding the flying squirrel by the tail beating it with a whip.

* * *

How do Russian women wring out their clothes?

They run them through the typewriter.

* * *

How do Russian women choose potato chips?

They pick the bag with contents that have settled the most. That way she's getting the most air for her money.

* * *

Why do Russian immigrants buy so many boxes of raisins?

They can't read English. They think its a box of dehydrated dog poop, "just add water!"

* * *

Then there was the smart old Russian who had a perfect way to diet.

He only eats when Germany wins a war.

Russian mattress: A Hefty trash bag filled with whipped cream.

* * *

Then there was the Russian who wanted to play his records but he couldn't afford a new needle for his can opener.

* * *

Why are Russian kids so mean?
You'd be mean too if you had to wear your sister's hand-me-down disposable diapers.

* * *

Are Russian women really fat?
I don't know but their high-heel shoes have shock absorbers.

* * *

Then there was the Russian in bell-bottom trousers who got arrested for letting his clapper hang out.

How does a Russian scientist study a vacuum?

He turns his head inside out and shoves it under a microscope.

* * *

Why are Russians so grouchy in the morning?

They spend an hour staring at the toaster waiting for the eggs to pop up.

* * *

What do you get when you cross a Russian eskimo with a swordfish?

I don't know . . . but don't ever rub noses!

* * *

Then there was the Russian who got so excited listening to Tom Jones sing "What's New Pussycat?" that he french kissed his angora and choked to death on a hair ball.

* * *

Then there was the Russian archaeologist who spent 20 years and 4 million dollars searching for the $10,000 pyramid.

The Soviets needed to come up with a good fertilizer to help them get better yields on their farms. They sent an agent to the US with orders to get some of America's finest manure and bring it back to the USSR.

He was arrested yesterday at a Dallas airport trying to smuggle two Texans in his suitcase.

* * *

And you heard about the Russian composer who died and couldn't make it as a ghost?

He couldn't find any "sheet" music.

* * *

Lord: "Excuse me, Adam, but I need to bother you for a rib.

Adam: "Why?"

Lord: "I want to make Woman."

Adam: "That's all?"

Lord: "Well, if you can spare that hemorrhoid I might make a Russian."

* * *

Russian after-dinner speech: "Burp!"

* * *

Volga Vulture: "I have a bone to pick with you!"

Boris Buzzard: "Really? Whose?"

Who carries the flag in a Russian parade?
The guy with the deepest belly button.

* * *

Russian in a shower: *The Naked Ape*.

* * *

Did you hear about the Russian messiah who brought a rabbit back to life?
It was a real "hare-raising" experience.

* * *

The Russians have a great Social Security program. Every year they take all the oldsters who turn 65, arm them to the teeth, and send them out to capture their own new country.

* * *

What do you find inside a Russian cereal factory?
A ton of stale cigarettes and a Veg-o-matic.

* * *

Did you hear about the Russian sabateur who did his job religiously?
He destroyed 8 priests, 4 nuns, a collection plate, and a church.

The Soviets have a no-waste attitude when it comes to farm products. Anything that grows, they use. They just introduced a new cereal to the people. It's called "Weedies."

* * *

Then there was Patronavich Wolfakov who went on a super strict diet. He wouldn't even kiss a girl unless she could prove she had diet saliva.

* * *

Ivan: "My brother-in-law has just been made commissariat in charge of public transportation."

Igor: "Think he can handle it?"

Ivan: "Sure. The city only has one problem right now."

Igor: "What's that?"

Ivan: "The elevators move sideways and the subway goes up and down."

* * *

Ivan: "Grandpa was running for freedom and a border guard shot him between the legs."

Igor: "Ouch! I'll bet that made him mad!"

Ivan: "Well, he did go off 'half-cocked'!"

Did you hear about the Russian peasant who stepped on a land mine? His funeral wreath read "Rest in Pieces!"

* * *

Who are the top three intellectuals in the Soviet Union?

Larry, Moe, and Curly Joe.

* * *

Russian singing group: The Lenin Sisters!

* * *

Then there was the mad Russian scientist who crossed a black dude with a codfish and got a filet-of-soul brother.

* * *

Are Russian basketball players good dribblers?

Only if they position their noses directly over the handkerchief.

* * *

Did you hear about the Russian champion in the pole vault?

He jumps over banks in Warsaw.

Why do Russians make disgusting guests at Halloween parties?

They bob for road apples.

* * *

And you heard about the Russian scientist who crossed a rabid dog with a rooster and got a feather duster that foams while it cleans.

* * *

At a diplomatic dinner the ambassadors were congregated discussing each country's superiority.

"We have the largest locks in the world!" said the representative of Panama

"But," interjected Japan's delegate, "we have the largest electronics industry in the world."

"And we," beamed the Russian, "have the largest bomb!"

"Well, uh, let's see, uh," stammered the US diplomat. "Have you guys ever seen Dolly Parton?"

* * *

Ivan: "My sister Katrina just made the Olympic boxing team."

Igor: "Fantastic! Do you think she'll make gold, silver, or bronze?"

Ivan: "Probably black and blue. She's a punching bag."

A Russian climber named Paul,
Gave scaling high mountains his all.
The state said "Go climb
Cause the summer's sublime."
And he died in the following fall.

* * *

How does a Russian father punish his son?
He takes away the keys to his tank.

* * *

Then there was the Russian schnook who got sent on an arctic expedition because his score on the government aptitude test was "absolute zero."

* * *

The owner of a beach resort was interviewing a Russian for the job of life guard. "Can you see well?" asked the interviewer.

"Yes."

"Are your arms and legs strong?"

"Yes."

"Then you're perfect! All you do is scan the water and swim out when someone goes down for the third time."

"Then I no be taking job!" cried the Russian. "I can only count to two!"

Russian astronaut Nicolai Brezenin just succeeded in identifying that cloud of mysterious pungent gas surrounding the North Pole. Would you believe Santa Claus farted?

* * *

Why do cannibals consider Russians such a great prize catch?

They make good dog food.

* * *

Why is the Soviet Union's population shrinking?

The guards keep shooting storks who try to violate their air space.

* * *

Did you hear about the mad scientist who crossed a Russian with a chicken and got a "Dumb Cluck?"

* * *

Two Russians were looking at photographs of the Grand Canyon.

"That's what we need in this country!" said the first.

"Yeah," agreed the second. "We could charge tourists to come over here and look at it!"

"I had a more practical use in mind."

"Such as?"

"Well, when we have our next purge it'd be a great place to bury the dead!"

* * *

Did you hear about the Russian scholar who got an honorary degree? From a thermometer!

* * *

Why wouldn't Noah let Russians on his ark?

He already had his quota of pigs.

* * *

And how about the Russian spider who was spinning his web in a crafts book and got so engrossed in the copy that he macramé-ed himself to death?

* * *

What is a Russian's favorite insect?

The assassin bug.

* * *

I guess you heard about poor Nicolas Detrevilich? He drowned while taking his pet oyster for a two-hour walk.

What is the number one cause of telephone malfunction in Russia?

Ear wax build-up.

* * *

A Russian scientist was sent to Africa to dig up the tomb of an ancient pharaoh. Twelve years went by and finally Moscow got impatient and wired the scientist.

HAVE YOU FOUND THE EGYPTIAN MONARCH? STOP WHAT'S THE HOLD UP? STOP REPLY AT ONCE STOP.

They soon received his reply:

HAVE FOUND MONARCH STOP HOW LONG DOES IT TAKE FOR THIS DAMN COCOON TO HATCH? STOP.

* * *

How do Russian coaches train their runners to jump so high?

They use barb-wire hurdles.

* * *

Did you hear about the Soviet scientist who spent six years searching for the Abominable Snowman?

He brought back three garbage bags full of frozen dandruff.

* * *

Why does Russia import more artificial limbs than any other nation?
They aren't all great saber dancers.

* * *

How do you recognize a Russian hobo in a flophouse?
He's the one nuzzling the bedbugs.

* * *

Why don't Russian women go to the beauty parlor?
The hair dryers won't fit over their army helmets.

* * *

How do you recognize a Russian at a banquet?
He's the hairy one eating mashed potatoes through a straw.

* * *

Russian merry-go-round: A revolving door.

How can you tell if a Russian just used your toilet?

It throws up.

* * *

How can you tell if you just kissed a Russian girl?

She'll be wearing vodka flavored lipstick.

* * *

Do Russian drivers run through red lights?

No, but they run *over* them a lot.

* * *

Did you hear about the Russian who went to Pizza Hut and bought a submarine?

It sank in his tub.

* * *

Ivan: "My sister's husband says he's related to Stalin!"

Igor: "The guy's a jackass!"

Ivan: "Hmmm! Then maybe he was telling the truth?"

An expert on cultural anthropology was addressing a group of his peers and made the statement that Russians as a people were dirty and disgusting.

"How can you make a broad statement like that?" jeered a Russian in the audience.

"Let me ask you a question," said the speaker. "Which hand do you use when you blow your nose?"

"My right one, of course!" answered the Russian.

"I thought so!" came the reply from the podium. "Most people use a handkerchief!"

* * *

How would you describe a Russian woman's mouth in one word?

"Gorge-ous!"

* * *

Did you hear about the Russian jockey who was shot trying to ride his horse across the Finnish line?

* * *

Why are there so few famous Russian painters?

It's so cold there that their finger paints keep freezing.

An American touring the Soviet Union couldn't resist the urge to pass a Bible to an old man.

"Take this, Brother," said the Yank. "It'll cleanse your soul."

"Thanks!" said the Russian. "But if it's all the same to you, I'll hang it in the outhouse and use it to cleanse something else."

* * *

The Russian government wastes almost as much money as ours. Only last year it spent $30,000,000 erecting Braille road signs for the blind.

* * *

Do they print Bibles in the Soviet Union?

Only on onionskin. Then they make adequate cigarette paper.

* * *

Why are Russian fortune tellers so disgusting?

They read toilet bowls.

* * *

Russian toilet powder: DDT.

Are Soviet traffic cops strict with foreign violators?

Yes! If they suspect you are driving while drunk, they'll ask you to walk a straight line . . . through a mine field.

* * *

How do you recognize a Russian at a cocktail party?

He's the one spearing olives with his bayonet.

* * *

Russian history lesson: The Bear facts!

* * *

Do Russian men have heavy beards?

Yes! Experts estimate that each contains 3.5 pounds of dirt.

* * *

Why do Russian farmers wear those big furry hats?

It cushions the blow when they step on rakes.

Where does a Russian keep his sheets and pillow cases?

In a Lenin closet.

* * *

Did you hear about the Russian kid who was going to spy school?

He gave his teacher an apple with a bomb in it!

* * *

Why is the Russian post office considered one of the worst in the world?

Because they fold the envelope, address the stamp, and lick the letters!

* * *

Are Russian women fat and hairy?

Yes. If they strip, put their hands behind their head, and open their mouths, they look like a hippopotamus in earmuffs.

* * *

Ivan: "What happened to you? You look like a bomb hit you!"

Igor: "Oh, I saw a land mine but it turned out to be a manhole cover."

Ivan: "So? What happened?"
Igor: "I dove under a manhole cover that turned out to be a land mine!"

*   *   *

Russian soft drink: A mattress soaked in vodka!

*   *   *

Russian graduation address: "Duh!"

*   *   *

Why can't Russian men get tattoos?
They slide off!

*   *   *

How can you pick a Russian out of a line-up?
He's the only guy not holding his nose.

*   *   *

Are Russians really empty headed?
Yes! Hit one on the noggin and he'll die from the echo.

Geologists have discovered the origins of the Soviet Union. It was created when Babe the Blue Ox relieved himself.

*   *   *

Then there was the Russian lass who was as pretty as a picture. Unfortunately it was Dorian Gray's.

*   *   *

Why does every Russian man carry a baseball mitt in his back pocket?

In case somebody across the street blows his nose.

*   *   *

Does the Soviet Union observe any of the same holidays as the US?

Sure! Every Valentine's Day they try and have at least one massacre.

*   *   *

Did you hear about the mad Russian scientist who crossed an Italian pontiff with an iceberg and got a "Pope-cycle."

Why don't Russian women bathe and shave their legs?

What? And put body lice on the endangered species list?

* * *

Then there was the Russian secretary who chopped up 4,392 pencils when her boss told her to "get the lead out!"

* * *

How does a Russian tie his shoes?
Together.

* * *

The world economic system has caught up with the Soviets too. They still plan on purging as usual, but they will be recycling the caskets.

* * *

How can Russians consume so much vodka and not have to rush to the toilet every few minutes?

Their belly buttons leak.

What's the difference between a taxi driver and a Russian track star?

Taxi drivers go fast and keep their meters running to make a living, and Russian track stars keep running meters fast to keep on living.

Thirty little green spacemen landed near Moscow. They toured the town and finally ended up in a restaurant. They were gunned down by a Russian cop as they marched across his table. He thought his salad was trying to run away.

*   *   *

Could a Russian movie star make it big in the US?
Only if Cheetah dies.

*   *   *

Did you hear about the fat Russian lady who took off all her clothes and went to a Halloween party as the Goodyear blimp with hair on it?

*   *   *

The mad Russian scientist has done it again. He crossed a Russian admiral with Charlie the tuna and got Chicken of the Red Sea.

*   *   *

Did you hear about the poor mosquito who bit a Russian and OD'd on vodka?

Is it true that Russian women give birth quickly and easily?

Yes! It's not at all unusual to be in a Moscow supermarket and see a lady's skirt move slightly and hear a baby scream "Geronimo!"

* * *

Why do most businesses prefer Russian cleaning ladies?

Because they can scrub with their armpits and save on steel wool.

* * *

Are Russian men really heavy spitters?

Well, let's put it this way: all Moscow dentists carry tidal wave insurance.

* * *

Then there was the Russian mad scientist who crossed an American football player with an English hunting dog and got a wide retriever.

* * *

What is the most reliable way to determine a Russian's age?

Saw him in half and count the rings of dirt.

Russian luxury cruise: A rubber army raft and two Volga boatmen grunting Rachmaninoff's greatest hits.

* * *

Do Russian movies gross very much in the Western world?

Oh, yes! The last one grossed out about 23 million people worldwide.

* * *

Did you hear about the Russian mad scientist who crossed a sadist with a magician and got a weirdo in a top hat that pulls the ears off rabbits?

* * *

How did the Russian Aladdin keep his genie from defecting to the West?

He put a safety cap on the bottle!

* * *

How do all Russian cowboy movies end?

The hero gets the girl, rides three-quarters of the way into the sunset, and turns back East at the barb wire fence.

Did you hear about the Russian who made a fortune selling barf bags during the Berlin air-lift?

*   *   *

How do you get rid of a Russian spy in New Mexico?

Call the Kremlin and tell them he was just elected President of the James Bond fan club.

*   *   *

What is the best selling shoe in the Soviet Union?

Cement overshoes.

*   *   *

President Carter was not the most popular president we've had according to *Pravda*. The Kremlin declared every Sunday "I Hate Jimmy" day and ordered every citizen to show their support by flushing a peanut butter sandwich down the toilet.

*   *   *

Why don't Russian immigrants make good Texans?

How do you expect a guy to remember the Alamo when he can't even remember to change his underwear?

A Westerner was touring Moscow and happened to see a bullet-riddled car with a "For Sale" sign on its shattered windshield. Seeing a Moscovite sitting on the curb nearby he asked: "Tell me, fellow, you don't really expect to sell that thing?"

"Why not?" asked the Russian. "It's a great deal. It was owned by a little old lady who only tried to cross the border on weekends."

Show me a Russian with his back to the wall and I'll show you a poor schmuck with his belly button to the firing squad.

*   *   *

It's not so surprising that the Soviets win so many track and field medals at the Olympic games. You'd be fast too if you'd spent most of your life dodging machine gun bullets.

*   *   *

Be careful when you shake hands with a Russian. He may try and jerk you a little closer to the border!

*   *   *

Then there was the mad Russian scientist who crossed a greyhound with a tank and got a bus that cocks its rear tire and blows away fire plugs.

*   *   *

How do you describe a romantic meal for two in Russia?
"Dinner by searchlight!"

Do they have a version of Humpty-Dumpty in Russia?

Certainly! Who do you think shot him off the wall?

* * *

4. Little Red Schoolhouse

Why don't Russian kids lose their report cards?
They're printed on flypaper.

* * *

Teacher: "Boris! Use the word 'offense' in a sentence."
Boris: "My aunt was gunned down as she tried to vault offense."

* * *

Then there was the Russian who spent 4 years in agriculture school learning how to grow dirt.

* * *

Then there was the Russian lightning bug who finished at the bottom of his class because he wasn't as "bright" as the other kids.

Then there was the Russian student who saw a doctor because his grammar teacher said he needed help with his colons and semicolons.

* * *

Those Russian kids from the University of Terrorism are really nuts! They're in a fad now to see who can blow up the telephone booth with the most people in it!

* * *

Did you hear about the Russian high-school kid who dyed his pubic hair light green?

He was the "sausage and sauerkraut" in the best ones possible.

* * *

Did you hear about the Russian high school kid who died his pubic hair light green?

He was the "sausage and saurkraut" in the senior-class play.

* * *

What do you call a Russian student who throws up on his books, wets in his chair, and soils his pants?

A Pugh-pil.

How are Russian school kids different from American school kids?

Russian school kids raise their hands to indicate that they've already *gone* to the bathroom.

* * *

What does a Russian teacher say to two fighting students?

"Okay, you two! Shake hands and make comrades!"

* * *

Did you hear about the Russian college kid who died trying to chug-a-lug a Molotov cocktail?

* * *

Why don't they have many high school dances in the Soviet Union?

It's hard to have fun with all those tanks chaperoning.

* * *

5. Kremlin Capers

How does a Russian VIP know he's in disfavor with the Party?

When the limousine that used to pick him up at the hotel is replaced by an ambulance.

* * *

Igor: "I think the Party is mad at me for something."

Ivan: "How do you know?"

Igor: "Last night the paper boy threw a grenade on my porch."

* * *

Did you hear about the Russian doll?

Wind it up and it runs for the border.

Igor: "Brezhnev hasn't got an enemy in the world!"

Ivan: "Since when?"

Igor: "Since 6 AM this morning. That's when he had the last of them shot."

* * *

Two Russian prisoners had been tied by the wrists and suspended from a beam in a Soviet dungeon. Hanging side-by-side for several weeks they had discussed every topic under the sun and one day the subject of matrimony came up.

"Were you ever married?" asked the first as he twisted his wrist to aid circulation.

"I thought about it several times," answered number 2. "But I always dreaded the thought of being *tied down.*"

* * *

The Russians have petitioned the US State Department for tissue samples. They were given permission to clone President Carter in their country. That way their ventriloquists will never run out of dummies.

* * *

President Brezhnev is not the world's best public speaker. Just the other night he went in to talk to his house plants and they were wearing ear plugs.

A Russian spider came home after a hard day of web mending. His wife grabbed him and made passionate love to him for nearly an hour.

"Wow!" exclaimed the surprised hubby. "Did you have a great day or what?"

"Oh, nothing special," cooed the female eight-legger. "But I did eat one Spanish fly."

* * *

A wicked dissenter named Boris
Yelled "the state doesn't do a thing for us!"
To yell was absurd
'Cause the state overheard
And made his whole abdomen porous!

* * *

Is the average Russian citizen aware of the number of political murders that take place in their country each day?

No. Most of them don't even read the sports pages.

* * *

A Russian political prisoner was captured by the KGB and given a horrible whipping. Looking over his shoulder at the bleeding stripes on his back he asked:

"Are you sure this is what all the political prisoners in Paris are wearing this year?"

The Russians are making a new TV show about a secret policeman and his three midget nudist sidekicks. It's called "Charlie's Cherubs."

* * *

Ivan: "Did you enjoy the speech made by Brezhnev last night?"
Igor: "Yes. I was afraid not to."

* * *

Russia is a very progressive country in some ways. For instance, capital punishment in this country involves capture, a long trial, extended incarceration on death row, months of appeals, retrials, and finally . . . *zap!* In Russia they don't waste time. Their executioners make house calls.

* * *

How do you recognize a lady secret policeman in Russia?
She's the one carrying a Howitzer in a shoulder holster.

* * *

Next time you're caught in a blizzard, don't despair. It might be two Russian spies sitting in a tree combing their hair.

Ivan: "What would you be if you weren't a communist?"

Igor: "Dead!"

* * *

How does the Russian secret police keep the citizens from phoning for help?

They put land mines in the Yellow Pages. And when their fingers do the walking . . . !

* * *

Teacher: "Boris! Use the word 'felon' in a sentence."

Boris: "My uncle was climbing over the wall, a guard shot him, then he felon died."

* * *

Natahsa: "You know, a lot of people are dying to get out of this country!"

Boris: "Yeah, and a lot of them who didn't make it are dead too."

* * *

Katrina: "We do not wish more children but those operations are so expensive."

Boris: "My brother got a vasectomy and it didn't cost him a thing."

Katrina: "Did you go to free government clinic?"

Boris: "No, he was trying to pole vault over barb wire on wall and missed."

What do the Russians do when a foreign dignitary visits Moscow?

They roll out the red toilet paper.

Did you hear about the Russian diplomat?

He sleeps in a *bunk* bed. Even when he eats at Colonel Sanders he's full of *bull*. He was fired from a sheep ranch for ripping the eyelids off twenty ewes while trying to pull the wool over their eyes. His favorite old-time radio actor is *Fibber* McGee. His favorite American rock singer is Sam the *Sham*. His favorite book is *Everything I know About Kissing* by Judas Iscariot. When he died the mortician charged double for making him look restful because he was two-faced.

* * *

Then there was the Russian agent who was ordered to get the president of the United States with a letter bomb.

At seven o'clock the next morning the "A" exploded on "Sesame Street."

* * *

Brezhnev had watched hundreds of hours of American television and was concerned that our more famous detectives might infiltrate his country. Elliot Ness, Kojak, Cannon, and other TV cops scared him to death. He called in his best agent and told him to go to the US and kill our most dangerous "flatfoot." He did. Disney studios announced this morning that they found Donald Duck with nine bullet holes in his body.

Then there was the Russian agent who was told to tail Orson Welles. He took along a ten-cent suppository in case he wanted to make a wish.

* * *

What do you call a Russian craps shooter who is caught in the act by the secret police and shot 95 times?

A "holey roller."

* * *

Last year the Kremlin ordered all television executives, technicians, and actors to be lined up outside their studios and shot. They called it a "TV pogrom."

* * *

Spy-nev: "Sir! President Carter's civil rights campaign is starting to affect the people. All of the Soviet citizens who like the American president are planning a coup tonight!"

Brezhnev: "So? Who's afraid of two people?"

* * *

Does the Russian government play games with its people?

Yes! It's called "Bang! Bang! You're dead!"

One thing that bothers a lot of folks about visiting big cities is there never seem to be enough taxis. You don't have to worry about that in Moscow. Just stand on the corner and yell, "communism stinks!" and they'll take you for a free ride.

* * *

Ivan: "Have you heard news? They be closing all bars on Election Day! We no be able to have vodka!"

Igor: "That's stupid! A guy'd have to be drunk out of his wits to vote for any of them in the first place."

* * *

Why are Russian diplomats like guns?
They're all large caliber "bores."

* * *

Ivan the terrible was auditioning new applicants for head executioner. One eager fellow approached the throne dragging a guillotine with two openings.

"That's novel!" cried the czar. "Why two openings?"

"Oh, that," explained the nervous job hunter. "Well, I also do mastectomies on weekends."

What's the difference between a Russian spy and a Jewish spy?

A Russian spy will put you in a cement overcoat. A Jewish spy will try to sell you a tie to go with it.

* * *

Then there's the Russian secret policeman who hangs the same sign on his door every day at noon: Out to Lynch.

* * *

Judge #1: "Nicolas! You must come to court tomorrow. I have a case you'll love to try!"

Judge #2: "Oh boy! Is it a political agitator?"

Judge #1: "No, it's 90-proof vodka!"

* * *

Eight Russian spies were being tried in a New England court. The case was decidedly controversial and so the court room was very noisy.

The judge banged his gavel and yelled, "Order, please!"

The eight Russians shouted, "Vodka!"

"It's really annoying when you think that only a year ago an Afghanistan tanker passed here every fifteen minutes!"

Why do Russian assassins kill in cold blood?
It's the only kind they have.

* * *

Are the Russian people ripe for revolt?
Well, some of them certainly smell ripe
. . . and they're among the most revolting
people I know.

* * *

Where are Russian secret papers kept?
Defiling cabinet.

* * *

Does the complexion of Russian politics
ever change?
Not unless Brezhnev has a pimple attack.

* * *

What did Nixon say to Eisenhower when
Cuba became a communist nation?
Well, there goes the hemisphere!"

* * *

Did you hear about the Russian spy they
caught near Woodstock?
He tried to infiltrate a rock festival in a tux-
edo.

Spy #1: "If Brezhnev doesn't take back what he said to me last night, I'm going to shoot myself!"

Spy #2: "What did he say?"

Spy #1: "He told me to shoot myself."

* * *

A pro golfer of some fame was invited to a White House function, and while milling through the crowd he ended up conversing with a Russian diplomat.

"Tell me," said the Soviet, "who is the winner in a game of your American golf?"

"Well," explained the pro, "it's really very complicated and I'm not going to get too technical, so just let me say that the winner is the fellow who gets the best lie."

"Oh, that's not complicated," said the Russian. "It's the same in the diplomacy game."

* * *

Did you hear about the Russian spy who killed himself with a pencil sharpener?

He was trying to sharpen his wits.

* * *

Igor: "Boy! Old Brezhnev almost bit off more than he could chew!"

Ivan: "You mean when he attacked Afghanistan?"

Igor: "No, I mean when he stuck the whole plug of tobacco in his mouth and they had to resuscitate him."

How does a Russian spy "bug" your phone?
He puts a tarantula in the receiver.

* * *

What is the longest book in Russia?
People I'm Gonna Kill by Josef Stalin.

* * *

Why are Russian spies so poor?
Their paychecks are signed in invisible ink.

* * *

Communist bloc: Little wooden building toy that Russian kids play with.

* * *

And you read about the dumb Russian infiltrator who disguised himself as a rose bush?
An alert White House gardener pruned him to death.

* * *

Did you hear about the Russian diplomat who got fired for operating without a Lie-cense?

Then there was the starving Russian spy who broke into a US dog food factory and was caught eating the contents of one of the vats.

He was shot down in his Prime.

* * *

Why is the Russian infant fatality rate so high?

They take their first step toward the border!

* * *

A Russian ambassador was taken on a tour of a progressive New England farm. He was seen taking meticulous notes while watching a milking machine in operation. Later that evening he told his aide at the embassy:

"It's true what we suspected about these Americans building mechanical livestock, Igor. This afternoon I watched them jump a cow."

* * *

Due to the number of American agents in the Middle East and Africa, Brezhnev ordered one of his spies to "clean up the area." It was a costly expedition. He's already used 4,592,412 gallons of Pledge dusting the Sahara desert!

You think the Russians don't have a definite elaborate plan for world domination? Ha! Brezhnev has his diary written for the next five years.

* * *

Brezhnev: "I understand Agent #1616 drowned after your liferaft was sunk by that US PT boat."

Agent: "Yes, sir. I told him to tie his pant legs together to make a float, but he forgot to take them off first!"

* * *

Boris: "Aren't you going to the anti-Carter rally at the Kremlin?"

Ivan: "Naw. I can't support it."

Boris: "But's he's an imperialist-capitalist American president!"

Ivan: "Yeah, but when you figure Truman and Eisenhower kept us out of Europe, Kennedy kept our missiles out of Cuba, Johnson kept us out of Vietnam, and Nixon kept us out of the Middle East, Jimmy's gift of Afghanistan makes him look like a pretty nice guy."

* * *

Brezhnev: "Did Spy #101764 get into the White House garden disguised as a tree?"

Agent: "Yes, but he isn't coming home."

Brezhnev: "What happened?"

Agent: "Forty dogs urinated on him and he didn't have a snorkel."

* * *

The Russian population is getting used to living in a police state where their lives are in constant danger. As a matter of fact, they are getting used to it to such a degree that seeing someone shot in the street doesn't bother them in the least. Only yesterday a car backfired in Moscow and 43 people turned around and yelled, "Nyah! Nyah! Ya missed me!"

* * *

Peter: "The police broke into my apartment last night and beat my wife."

Boris: "Did they get anything out of her?"

Peter: "If they did they cleaned it up before I got home."

* * *

Ivan: "I don't care if he is our country's best spy, I'm not going all the way to America just to get him off the hook."

Boris: "Yeah! He shouldn't have been swimming around in that lake trying to eat worms anyway."

Then there was the Russian prisoner who sat on an egg for six years trying to hatch an escape plot.

Brezhnev: "Well? Did you get our agent out of that Arizona jail?"

Spy-guy: "No, your dictatorship. I failed."

Brezhnev: "Didn't you use fool-proof escape plan like we saw in US Western films we stole?"

Spy-guy: "Yes, sir. I backed my horse to the jail window and tied one end of the rope to my saddle and tossed the other end through the window and galloped off."

Brezhnev: "So? What went wrong?"

Spy-guy: "He tied his end of the rope around his neck."

* * *

Soccer is a big spectator sport in Russia. Every year Brezhnev attends the first game of the season and throws out the first dissenter.

* * *

An American had made a good friend during the world competition, and one day he saved up enough money to visit his friend in the Soviet Union. After a two-week stay it was time to leave. "I'd like to do something for you before I leave," said the US athlete. "Anything. You name it."

"I would, comrade," said the Russian runner. "But it is too dangerous."

"Please," begged his American chum. "Tell me. I'll try."

"Well," answered the Russian, "we are oppressed, and just once before I die I would like to write what I really feel about this regime."

"You wait my friend!" urged the American. "One day you will get your wish!"

And it took nearly a year, but he was true to his word. He hired a band of mercenaries to accompany him back to the Soviet Union, and in a bloody battle that cost him an eye and an arm he managed to get his friend aboard a plane to freedom. After fighting off attacking Soviet planes and a hazardous flight to the US, he bought his friend a small weekly paper and set him up in the publishing business.

"There!" he beamed, full of humanitarian pride. "You have your life's wish!"

"Could I ask you one more small favor, comrade?" asked the Russian.

"Certainly," replied his friend.

"Well . . . could you teach me to write?"

* * *

Two Russians were sneaking through the woods to meet a plane that was to fly them to freedom in the West. "With my luck," muttered the first, "this will be some fly-by-night airline!"

"I hope so," said the second. "If we try it during the day some MIG will shoot us down!"

Igor: "My cousin was shot trying to cross the border disguised as a sheep."

Ivan: "Too bad. What are you putting on his tombstone?"

Igor: " 'Here Lies A Died-In-The-Wool Communist'!"

* * *

Then there was the Russian secret agent who was ordered to sabotage America's grease production, so he tried to shoot John Travolta and Olivia Newton John.

* * *

Is it true that Russians are a race of chronic liars?

Well, Pinocchio took a course in Russian diplomacy and his nose exploded.

* * *

Ivan is the super spy!
He's mean and ruthless, tough and sly,
Ugly, dirty, dumb, and loud.
No wonder he makes the Kremlin proud.

Ivan is without a doubt
The cruelest spy there is about.
He's a case! A real baddie!
Even swamp rats call him "Daddy!"

*   *   *

There once was an agent named Nickie,
Who was ruthless and vile and tricky!
He'd break into homes
And bug all the phones.
I think he took lessons from Dickie!

*   *   *

Russian telephone call:
Operator: "The number you have dialed has been disconnected. The building the phone was in has been disintegrated. The party you are calling has disappeared. Please ask your local Party policeman for assistance."

*   *   *

How can you recognize a diplomat who just dealt with a Russian?
He's the guy with the knife in his back.

How can you tell if an escaped Russian spy has fled through the swamp?

The alligators have clothespins on their noses.

Two Russian spies had just stolen a book of children's nursery rhymes, and believing it to be top secret documents, hurried to their hide-out to read it.

"I got good news and bad news," said the first as he finished the book. "The good news is London Bridge is falling down and Bo Peep lost her sheep. The bad news is their cow just jumped over *our* moon!"

* * *

Igor: "Sometimes I think this communist thing is a bunch of hooey!"

Ivan: "What in particular?"

Igor: "Like sharing everything equally."

Ivan: "Aw! Six families to an apartment isn't so bad."

Igor: "Yeah, but you'd think they'd give us more than one sheet of toilet paper!"

* * *

How does the Russian propaganda office get information to the people?

They tell a woman and swear her to secrecy.

* * *

Natasha: "Darlink! Take me to Spain to the bullfight! Russia is so dull. There is no matador! There is no bull!"

Boris: "What do you mean 'no bull!'? Didn't you hear Brezhnev's speech last night?"

Igor: "The state sure is determined to do my cousin Stanislov in."

Ivan: "Why? What happened?"

Igor: "They assigned him to a new job. He works all day in the deep, dark, and damp where the air is most foul."

Ivan: "You mean the coal mines in Donetsk?"

Igor: "No. They made him a gynecologist in Moscow."

* * *

How can you recognize a communist drunk in a bar?

He's the one that sees *red* elephants.

* * *

A tourist was in the car of a Moscow tour guide.

"Stop at this building," asked the tourist. "I'd like to see it."

"Can't. Top secret."

"Oh, sorry. How about that museum over there?"

"Can't. Top secret."

"Could we go to the big building with the gold spires?"

"Nope. Top secret."

"Listen! Is there anywhere I can go that isn't top secret?"

"That depends. Do you have to go Number One or Number Two?"

Ivan: "Welcome back from prison, comrade. What did you do to get sent away?"

Igor: "I stole some papers."

Ivan: "Ah! Top secret? From the Kremlin?"

Igor: "No. Toilet. From the men's room."

* * *

Two Russians had just arrived at a top security prison. As they were being led through the courtyard one started getting very excited.

"Look!" he exclaimed to the other prisoner. "That wall must be at least fifteen feet high and a hundred yards long."

"So what?" retorted the second. "A wall is a wall."

"Oh, but comrade," exclaimed the first. "This is a fine wall!"

"What are you? Crazy?"

"No! I'm a handball enthusiast. What a wall!"

* * *

Ivan: "My Uncle Peter bumped into a wall and died."

Igor: "What was he doing?"

Ivan: "Getting shot."

* * *

Did you hear about the Russian who tried to sneak across the border disguised as a stein of beer?

The guard got him with a "mug shot."

"Pardon me, sir," said the customs official to a Russian and his family who were entering this country, "but I have to inspect your bags."

"You can inspect my wife," replied the Moscovite. "But you leave my mother alone!"

* * *

Igor: "Hey! Is your brother still pushing for reform?"

Ivan: "No. Now he's pushing up daisies."

* * *

A KGB agent was assigned to the State of Florida to collect intelligence information. One weekend he decided to go for a swim in the warm ocean waters. He hadn't been in the water for five minutes when an electric eel clamped down on his left leg, a shark bit off his right leg, and a Portuguese Man-of-War wrapped itself around his neck and stung him. The KGBer managed to wrestle his way free and make it to shore where he took a radio out of his trunks and called Moscow: "Moscow?" he gasped. "This be agent 468-32! Their interrogation techniques are a bit unorthodox, but don't worry. I didn't tell them nothing!"

* * *

How do Russian diplomats do on TV appearances?

Not so good on "Face the Nation." Terrific on "Liar's Club."

Why do the Russians send all veterinarians to Siberia?

Because they have over 2,000,000 sled dogs and somebody has to change their antifreeze.

* * *

Do concentration camp guards in Russia let the prisoners have any recreation?

Sure! They get to play Russian roulette anytime they want to!

* * *

He-kov: "My brother is sure living high these days."

She-kov: "Oh, did the Party promote him?"

He-kov: "No, they shot him into space."

* * *

Russian nursery Rhyme:

Mary had a little lamb.
Its fleece was white as snow.
He tried to jump the barb wire fence
And a sentry laid him low!

You've heard of Russian voodoo? That's when the secret police beat your face until it resembles their doll and poke bayonets in you until the doll dies.

* * *

How does a Russian spy telephone a Chinese spy?
He dials the Wong number.

* * *

There is no free speech in Russia. Even their most popular cereal goes "snap, crackle and sh-h-h-h-h-h!"

* * *

I think the Russian subversives are at it again. Last night my wife found a spy ring in the tub.

* * *

Is the average Russian citizen brainwashed? Yes! But the rest of him . . . *pugh!*

Two Russian diplomats were attending a play in New York. Feeling the need to use the men's room they began searching for it. They soon found themselves backstage and outside the star's dressing room.

"Oll, comrade!" beamed one. "A star on this door!"

"Gee!" said the second. "I knew there were a lot of communist party members in this country but I didn't know there were enough to need separate restrooms!"

* * *

Is life in a communist country really as harsh and dangerous as they say?

Yep! As a matter of fact, infant stores in Moscow offer bullet-proof vests in pink or blue!

* * *

Why does Russia send all its midgets to Siberia?

Because they have so many death certificates to fill out daily that they need folks who can take shorthand.

* * *

Are people in Moscow very sociable?

Sure! Just yell "The Party stinks!" and they'll give you a spontaneous necktie party!

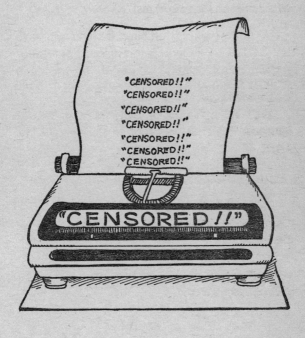

OFFICIAL RUSSIAN TYPEWRITER

Rusky: "I would like to come to USA and give speech on the benefits of communism."

Agent: "I should warn you that the audience will give you a lot of raspberries."

Rusky: "I admit it's not much pay, but what the heck. I love fruit."

* * *

If you're looking for bargains you can save lots of money shopping in Russia. Some poor merchant somewhere is sure to be having a "Going to Siberia Forever" sale.

* * *

Why are the drains always plugged up in Moscow?

People keep trying to use them for escape tunnels.

* * *

Do they have a free press in Russia?

No! They charge for subscriptions like everybody else.

Mrs. Lamatov died today at age 43. Her husband was a prisoner in Siberia and she tried to bake him a cake with a bomb in it.

* * *

How do you get rid of a communist spy in Mississippi?

Sell him the tar-and-feathers concession at a Klan rally.

* * *

How do you get rid of a communist spy in Detroit?

Give him a new Ford Pinto that goes 80 mph in reverse!

* * *

Did you hear about the communist hit-man who was ordered to kill a 10-year-old kid?

He put cherry-bombs in the bubble gum machine to make it look like an accident.

Khrushchev wasn't such a dumb guy. Sure, he banged a good pair of dress shoes on the UN podium, but he also owned all the shoe repair stores in Russia!

* * *

Russian birthday parties are a blast! As soon as you light the candles on the cake, fifteen secret policemen jump out, yell "Surprise," and blow you away.

* * *

How can you tell if you're driving through Siberia?

The traffic signs say "Mush" and "Don't Mush!"

* * *

He-ski: "I think we're gonna start celebrating Thanksgiving!"

She-ski: "Really?"

He-ski: "Yes! I heard Brezhnev say he'd love to gobble up Turkey!"

* * *

Then there was the mad Russian scientist who crossed a gorilla with a roll-on deodorant and got a "Secret policeman."

Did you hear about the grocer in Moscow who was eliminated because his Rice Krispies talked too much?

* * *

Ivan: "My Uncle Tetlaich is thinking of becoming a politician."

Igor: "Is he a member of the Party?"

Ivan: "No. He's for a free society and the end of communism."

Igor: "Wow! What's he running for? I'll vote for him!"

Ivan: "Last time I saw him he was running for his life."

* * *

Russian political rally: Two drunken Bolsheviks booing Radio Free Europe.

* * *

Ivan: "See these scars on my chest? I once ran for the border."

Igor: "Wow! Did they shoot you?"

Ivan: "No, stupid! I was born with 85 bullet holes in my body!"

Ivan: "My brother-in-law was questioned by the secret police."

Igor: "What kind of questions did they ask?"

Ivan: "Multiple choice."

Igor: "You mean like choosing answer a, b, or c?"

Ivan: "No, I mean Multiple Choice. If he didn't answer correctly they gave him multiple fractures on choice parts of his body."

* * *

Ivan: "I don't understand it! The communists won again. I gave the people an alternate choice."

Igor: "Maybe it was your platform they objected to."

Ivan: "Why? I only advocated a return to a monarchy."

Igor: "Yes, but 'Two czars in every garage' was a bit much."

* * *

Natasha: "Oh, Boris! I so sorry! I just burn turkey!"

Boris: "Sorry? Why sorry? Those Moslem trouble-makers deserved it!"

Did you hear about the anticommunist politician in the Soviet Union? He would have won in a landslide if he hadn't lost in that rockslide.

* * *

Why are Russian dissenters like Quaker Oats?
They're both "shot from guns."

* * *

The Soviet government disapproves of popular music because crowds tend to gather to hear it performed. But they solved the problem. They took 10,000 prison inmates, gave them sledge hammers, and told them to break big rock concerts into little ones.

* * *

Then there was the Russian spy who was caught trying to hypnotize Smoky the Bear into playing with matches.

* * *

6. In the Pinko

A Russian had just gotten back from a stint in Siberia and had gone to a dentist for help with his cavities.

"Tsk! Tsk!" said the doc. "These are in bad shape!"

"They oughta be!" said the patient. "For the last 30 years they've been chattering 24 hours a day!"

* * *

A bald-headed doctor named Larry
Tried to turn his bare pate into hairy.
But his serum brought pain,
Ate his skin, skull, and brain,
So there's only this body to bury.

A major league US baseball team traveled to the Soviet Union to play their newly formed club. During the game a US base runner was hit by a thrown ball as he tried to steal. The Russian infielders and pitcher stood calmly by and watched the player bleed terribly from the nose.

"Hey!" screamed the US manager as he ran onto the field. "Why don't you give that man first aid?"

"Because, stupid," explained the Soviet pitcher. "He was on his way to second!"

* * *

Boris: "Can you help me, doctor? I fear the whole world is out to get me!"

Doc: "Nonsense! Red China and NATO maybe, but not the whole world."

* * *

A serious contagious disease broke out in a Moscow neighborhood. A city health official told all those who were ill to board a special train that would transport them all in an isolated car to the hospital on the other side of town.

"How about tickets?" inquired a victim. "We'll need tickets."

"Don't worry," said the health inspector. "Just stick out your tongue and show the horrible green coating and the conductor will let you aboard."

The train arrived at its destination but nobody got off. The health inspector hopped aboard and found one still conscious man coughing blood.

"Good grief, comrade!" cried the health man. "What happened!"

"The tickets!" gasped the suffering Russian. "The idiot conductor tore them all in two!"

* * *

Why can't Russians use crutches?
The sweat in their armpits eats off the ends.

* * *

Why can't Russians use band-aids?
They slide off!

* * *

How do psychiatrists mold a Russian's personality?
They cover it with yeast and put it in a warm moist place.

An American diplomat was involved in a traffic accident while in Moscow. Coming to in the hospital he was told that a transfusion had saved his life.

"Where's the donor?" asked the grateful recipient. "I'd like to thank him."

"You can send him doggie treats in care of city kennel," replied the Russian nurse.

"A dog!" screamed the incredulous American. "You used a dog!"

"Oh, don't worry!" cooed the nurse. "He be honest-to-God bloodhound!"

* * *

Did you hear about the absent-minded Russian pharmacist? He kept putting the "shake well" labels on the nitroglycerin bottles. He was under such terrific tension at the lab that he was always ready to explode. But his fellow workers didn't mind. . . . They got a real bang out of it. He's the original member of the "Hole-in-the-Wall Gang."

* * *

Why are Russians eagerly sought by poison treatment centers?

Everywhere they go they induce vomiting.

Did you hear about the Russian doctor who died trying to restrain a karate expert with muscle spasms?

Then there was the idiot Russian doctor who put a vampire on a liquid diet.

* * *

A Russian diplomat was ordered by his doctor to take a vacation on a South Sea island to get away from it all. Knowing the man was on the verge of a mental breakdown, the physician had sent along his assistant to be sure the trip was restful and rejuvenating. Two weeks later the assistant called Moscow and reported the man was dead.

"Dead?" exclaimed the doctor. "What happened?"

"Well," explained the assistant, "we saw a red starfish on the beach, and that reminded him of the Party. Then we saw a tall palm tree swaying in the breeze, and that reminded him of the guard towers. And finally when we saw a decomposing whale on the beach, that reminded him of his wife . . . and he blew his brains out!"

* * *

Did you hear about the Russian whose doctor told him to go home and "lay down on the sofa?"

He ripped the feathers off his duck and lay them on the sofa.

Then there was the Russian nurse who had bedpan hands.

* * *

How can you recognize a hospital zone in Moscow?

The guards all have silencers on their machine guns.

* * *

Doc #1: "Hey, that Russian lady had that baby a week ago. Shouldn't she be going home?"

Doc #2: "Naw. We have to keep her a few more days."

Doc #1: "Why? Did she have a difficult delivery?"

Doc #2: "Sort of. She had one giant contraction and swallowed her cigar."

* * *

Then there was the Russian scientist who spent 20 years living in the jungle with gorillas. All he got were two cases of incurable African VD and a paternity suit.

You know what a Russian cold is, right?
It sort of "creeps up" on you.

* * *

A European tourist had a ruptured appendix and went to a Moscow hospital for emergency surgery. When he came out of the anesthesia, he noticed the bed beside his contained a body with no arms or legs. When the nurse came he had to ask, "This guy next to me, did he have gangrene?"

"No," replied the Soviet sister. "He had tattoos and we had to censor them."

* * *

What type of gas do they use in a Russian operating room to put you out?

The nurse removes her blouse and fans her armpits.

* * *

Then there was the Russian breast surgeon who was arrested for going around Moscow offering all the ladies free inspections and estimates.

Ivan: "How did your sister's plastic surgery come out?"

Igor: "She's as ugly as ever."

Ivan: "Didn't they graft new skin onto her face?"

Igor: "Yes. But she used to be cossack and the skin they took from her rump and put on her face contained fourteen saddle sores."

* * *

Why do Russian girls take so long getting ready for dates?

They don't want to rush their plastic surgeons.

* * *

How does a Russian doctor deliver a breech baby?

First he gets a tractor and a long chain . . .

* * *

What do you call a bandage from a Soviet hospital?

A Russian dressing.

Why do Russian surgeons always finish their operations by 12 noon?

That's when the cafeteria wants their silverware back.

* * *

What makes Russian dentists so despised?

I think it's the goldfish they mold new teeth out of.

* * *

What does a Russian doctor do before he takes out your appendix?

He buys it a corsage and makes dinner reservations for two.

* * *

Why are Russian surgeons so disgusting?

Instead of a sponge they use a bread and butter pusher.

* * *

Then there was the spy who went to the doctor because he had a code in his nose.

Then there was the Russian who paid $1,000,000 for a kidney stone to finish his rock collection.

* * *

What is the most dreaded disease in the Soviet Union?
"Boob-onic" plague.

* * *

Did you hear about the Russian spy who died of lung cancer trying to infiltrate Marlboro Country?

* * *

Did you hear about the Russian girl who had a nose job?
It grew back.

* * *

Did you hear about the Russian eskimo lady who drowned during menopause?
She had one big hot flash in her sleep and the igloo melted.

How many Russian doctors does it take to give a lady her prenatal exam?

Five. Four to hold her up to the light bulb and one to see if the baby is developing.

A frustrated doctor called a pharmacist who attended to the needs of the Russian immigrants in his neighborhood.

"Charlie?" said the doctor. "This is Evans at Community Hospital. We just operated on fourteen more Russians today. It's the Cert problem again. Are you still selling those people Certs?"

"Sure," answered the pharmacist. "I keep telling them 'Certs is a breath mint' and 'Certs is a candy mint.' Is it my fault if they use it as a suppository?"

*   *   *